DATE DUE

BUCK WILD

BUCK WILD

HOW REPUBLICANS BROKE THE BANK AND
BECAME THE PARTY OF BIG GOVERNMENT

STEPHEN SLIVINSKI

NELSON CURRENT

A Subsidiary of Thomas Nelson, Inc.

Published in Nashville, Tennessee, by Nelson Current, a division of a
wholly-owned subsidiary (Nelson Communications, Inc.) of Thomas Nelson,
Inc.

Nelson Current books may be purchased in bulk for educational, business,
fundraising, or sales promotional use. For information, please e-mail
SpecialMarkets@ThomasNelson.com.

Library of Congress Cataloging-in-Publication data
on file with the Library of Congress.

ISBN: 1-59555-064-X

Printed in the United States of America

06 07 08 09 10 QW 5 4 3 2 1

For my mother and father

"One of my jobs as President is to make sure we keep fiscal sanity in the budget."

GEORGE W. BUSH

31 August 2001

CONTENTS

CONTENTS

FROM THE CESSPOOL
TO THE HOT TUB

The Era of Super-Sized Government

I t sounds like a bad joke, even by Washington standards.

How many genuine fiscal conservatives are left in the Republican Party?

Punch line: Not enough to fill a small, dank, windowless room in the basement of the Longworth House Office Building on Independence Avenue.

That's where, in early May 2004, a small band of Republican congressmen met to lament the fiscal profligacy that characterized the modern GOP. Once upon a time, the group would meet in the ornate rooms of the Capitol building or even the cushy splendor of the Speaker's office. Now they meet in a basement like a band of insurgents. All they lack is a password and a secret handshake.

The meeting attendees were some of the core members of a group called the Republican Study Committee. In the shorthand of DC political wonks, they are known as the RSC. The group was created in 1973 by conservatives in the House of Representatives who wanted to declare their independence from President Richard Nixon who, with the assistance of House minority leader Gerald Ford, was cutting deals with the big spenders in Congress.

The RSC banded together again when George H.W. Bush

broke his "no new taxes" pledge. They revolted—albeit un-successfully—against the budget that Bush had brokered with Democrats which led to one of the biggest tax hikes in US his-tory. The fight put them at odds with many senior Republicans who supported Bush's scheme.

Today, over thirty years after its inception, the RSC still exists. Its members continue to be alienated by a Republican presi-dent who—with the aid and even encouragement of many Republicans in Congress—has embraced Big Government and expanded the welfare state beyond the dreams of even the most starry-eyed liberal Democrat.

It's funny how history repeats itself.

The historical parallels weren't lost on the attendees of the May 2004 basement meeting. Some of them, like Jeb Hensarling of Texas, were among the newest members of Congress, motivated to come to Washington to fight for the principles of limited government. Other attendees were more senior but still committed to the same vision, like John Shadegg of Arizona, then the chairman of the RSC. The son of Stephen Shadegg, long-time friend and speechwriter of Barry Goldwater, John was first elected to Congress ten years earlier in what became known as the "Republican Revolution." He was among the last of a dwindling breed. Of the seventy-three House GOP freshmen who stormed Capitol Hill after the historic electoral victory of 1994, less than half were still serving in the House ten years later.

A few of the Republican Revolutionaries were still in Congress, but on the other side of the Capitol, as senators. Others had decided it was just too tough to win a fight against the forces of Big Government and had left. Others eventually had been defeated for reelection. Still others kept their vow to return to civilian life after serving no more than a few terms. And when their congressional careers were over, these former members of Congress didn't have much to show for their valiant efforts. Mark Sanford—current governor of South Carolina and one of the House members who kept his promise to serve only three terms—summed up the sentiments of many fellow conservatives shortly before he left office in 1999: "[You] would hate to say that you spent six years of your life at a job and at the end of it government was spending more and taxing more than when you came. But that's where we are."[1]

It wasn't supposed to be like this.

Republicans had won some fights against the big spenders after winning control of Congress in 1994. But congressional leaders retreated from the battle for smaller government after only two years in the majority.

Then, in 2000, the Republicans won united control of Congress and the White House, a feat the party had not accomplished since the 1952 elections. Many conservatives and supporters of limited government believed that smaller government—a Republican promise since Ronald Reagan sat in the Oval Office—was just around the corner.

Instead, the drive to scale back the federal government sputtered and died. Historic budget surpluses turned into deficits. The president and the congressional GOP leadership—all of whom still publicly claimed to be in favor of limiting government—expanded government faster than at any time since the 1960s.

While the RSC members were meeting in a basement that spring day in 2004 to discuss how to slap some sense into their party brethren, President George W. Bush was running for reelection by standing proudly on a record of huge increases in the size of government. Press release after press release from the Bush-Cheney campaign boasted of the two major expansions of Big Government it had engineered: the brand-new and fabulously expensive drug benefit in Medicare—the biggest expansion of that program since its inception in the 1960s—and the doubling of the budget of the Department of Education, a cabinet agency twice slated for extinction in the heady days of the Reagan and Gingrich revolutions.

To many fiscal conservatives—then as now—it seems the biggest impediments to change are no longer the Democrats in Congress. Instead, the enemies are Republicans on Capitol Hill and in the White House. Gone are the days of victories, moral or otherwise, over Big Government. As one *Los Angeles Times* reporter put it: "No longer are Republicans arguing with Democrats about whether government should be big or small. Instead they are at odds over what kind of big government the US should have."[2] Former speaker of the House, Newt Gingrich lamented to a *New York Times* reporter: "Republicans have lost their way."[3]

Supporters of smaller government cheered when President Clinton declared in his 1996 State of the Union address, "The era of big government is over." Today it has been replaced by something far worse: the era of super-sized government. And for that we have the Republicans to thank.

By the summer of 2005, the members of the RSC—that

group of rebels who were convening in a basement on a beautiful spring day in 2004—would begin fighting their own party leaders in an attempt to steer the GOP back to the principles of limited government. That fight may end up defining the Republican Party for years to come.

A PARTY OF SMALL GOVERNMENT NO MORE

The fiscal damage of the George W. Bush years is an awful legacy for the Republican Party to stand by as they head into a critical set of congressional and presidential elections. Total federal government spending grew by 45% in Bush's first term. After adjusting the total growth in the federal budget by length of time in office and inflation, so far George W. Bush is the biggest spending full-term president since Lyndon B. Johnson.

In terms of spending on domestic programs, Bush looks less like Reagan and more like Nixon, another Republican president who prided himself on expanding government dramatically. Defense spending has shot up, too. But much of the Bush defense build-up is not related to the war on terror, the invasion of Afghanistan, or the war in Iraq.

Bush has not been alone in the spending binge, of course. The Republican-controlled Congress has been fully complicit and indeed bears much of the blame since it controls the purse strings. The GOP congressional majority started out strong in its first few years. It made some progress in downsizing the federal government by cutting spending for the first time since Ronald Reagan was in office. Yet, even these small victories were short-lived. Just one year after the GOP took control of

Congress, spending on domestic programs began to creep upward again.

Voters have been getting increasingly disgusted with the Republicans. In March 2004, the George Washington University *Battleground* poll revealed that 47% of the likely voters surveyed believed that the Democrats in Congress would do a better job than the Republicans at "holding down federal spending." Only 42% thought Republicans would be better. In other words, over half of those polled were registering a vote of "no confidence" in the ability of the GOP to shrink government, a promise the GOP was so strongly connected with in the public mind for at least the past twenty-five years. Since the 2004 elections, the poll numbers have only gotten worse for the GOP. By February 2006, only 33% of likely voters trusted Bush to keep the spending down, and only 36% trusted Republicans in Congress to do so.[4]

A GOP defender might argue that these polls are skewed in favor of those who are already hostile to Republican fiscal policy. Yet, in each of these polls, Republicans were trusted by more than 50% of the respondents to keep taxes low. In other words, many of the same people who trust Republicans to cut taxes—and who tend to like Republicans for that reason—don't think the GOP will stop its spending binge.

These poll results are not anomalies, either. Other polls show a similar decline in the approval ratings of Republicans on budget issues. The *Wall Street Journal* reported that its poll, taken in conjunction with NBC News, found that voters felt Democrats could control spending better.[5] In fact, Democrats had a twelve-point edge (34% for the Democrats versus 22% for the GOP). The last time such a margin existed was in 1994 and 1995. Republicans came out on top in those polls.

It's not that the Democrats have shrugged off the mantle of big-spending liberalism. They haven't, and they probably won't. What the polls seem to be saying is this: In the minds of a majority of likely voters, the Grand Old Party is no longer a serious alternative for voters who want to restrain government.

MANY VOTERS DON'T LIKE BIG GOVERNMENT

If Republicans have an image problem, it's of their own making. An administration and a congressional majority that were finally supposed to make some lasting headway in the battle *against* Big Government have instead built a party *of* Big Government. Voters are now stuck with a choice between the party of Big Government (the Republicans) and the party of Even Bigger Government (the Democrats).

Yet many people seem to prefer another option: a party of smaller government. More than a majority of people, when asked, just don't seem to like Big Government. Polling expert Karlyn Bowman compiled all the results from ABC News/ *Washington Post* polls and CBS News/ *New York Times* polls going back to the mid-1970s.[6] Each poll included a version of this question: "If you had to choose, would you rather have a smaller government providing fewer services or a bigger government providing more services?" Notice the general upward trend in those who prefer smaller government in the following figure.

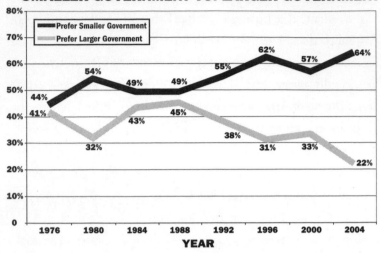

SMALLER GOVERNMENT VS. LARGER GOVERNMENT

Pollster Scott Rasmussen asked a similar poll question in February 2004 and found that 64% of Americans said they prefer smaller government with fewer services and lower taxes.[7] Perhaps the most surprising finding in his poll was that this preference cuts across virtually all demographic lines. Men prefer it (67%), and so do women (62%). The majority of people over the age of 30 do (52%), and even more of those over 65 do also (70%). Most Republican voters do (79%), and so do a majority of Democrats (53%). Even the racial divide doesn't seem so unbridgeable when you discover that 61% of white voters prefer smaller government, as do 52% of nonwhite voters. The only exception to this pattern is voters who identify themselves as "very liberal," and even then, 40% of them prefer smaller government.[8]

The Gallup polling company has been asking people an interesting question since the 1960s: Which institution do you consider to be the biggest threat to the country—Big Government, Big Business, or Big Labor (a.k.a. labor unions).[9] Big Labor doesn't register much anymore. But Big Government has been seen as the biggest threat by 50% or more of Americans in virtually every year since 1983. Between 1995 and 2000, around 65% of Americans consistently regarded Big Government as the biggest threat.

Big Business has been in the 20% range for most of the past forty years, except for 2002 when, at the height of the Enron scandal, it was seen as the biggest threat to the country by 38% of respondents. However, Big Government was still seen as an even bigger threat that year by 47% of those polled. Once the Wall Street scandals passed, the threat rankings for business sank back to the mid-20s, while Big Government hopped right back up to 57% in 2004.

It seems there is a large constituency that would respond favorably to a political party that can enunciate a clear program to make the federal government smaller, less powerful, and less intrusive. It's those sorts of voters—Republicans, Democrats, and independents alike—who catapulted Reagan to the White House. Those voters are still up for grabs. The GOP cannot take them for granted anymore.

THE CESSPOOL BECOMES A HOT TUB

A slow de-evolution of the GOP began once the party won a majority in Congress. Instead of advancing the cause of smaller government, the Republicans eventually regressed into a party devoted solely to tightening their grip on political power, without regard to the principles that hoisted them to majority status in the first place. The GOP today has largely made peace with the federal programs it once wanted to end.

When speaking to conservative audiences, elected Republicans wave the flag of smaller government. But behind the scenes, they have already effectively surrendered the battle. Sure, Big Government is bad, they admit in private, but only when the other guys are in charge. When Republicans are at the helm, they can rationalize keeping Big Government around. They think everything will be all right as long as they are the ones holding the reins.

Look at the budgets the Republicans have proposed and enacted over the past five years and you will discover that they don't resemble a platform for stripping government down to size. Instead, they resemble something that late-night huckster Matthew Lesko would devise. You might recognize Lesko as the man infamous for the commercials in which he wears a jacket adorned with giant question marks. In these commercials, he hawks the books he has published—titles like *Gobs and Gobs of Free Stuff* and *Free Money for Everyone*. The most recent edition of his book, *Free Money to Change Your Life*, runs over 1,000 pages. The books contain extensive lists of federal programs that dispense your tax money. Paging through them gives you a hint of how vast and expensive the federal government has grown. Republicans have eagerly hastened that growth.

Ronald Reagan liked to work a fable into some of his speeches. It went something like this: When fiscal conservatives look at Washington DC, they see a cesspool. When they are elected on the promise of changing the system, they finally get to the nation's capital and are soon seduced by Big Government. Suddenly, Washington no longer seems like a cesspool. Now it seems more like a hot tub.

This book is an attempt to make some sense of how Washington DC started to feel like a hot tub to so many members of the Republican Party. It does not endeavor to deliver an authoritative history of the GOP over the past twenty-five years. Rather, it seeks to discover how the party of Reagan—once guided by the promise of cutting government back to its core constitutional functions—eventually lost its head. It aims to put the current Republican tailspin into context by recounting critical episodes that spurred the transformation of the GOP into the party of Big Government.

This book will also explore some important questions that should be considered by anyone who prefers smaller government to the hulking behemoth we have now. For instance, would a Republican loss of the White House or Congress in an upcoming election be a bad thing for fiscal conservatives? It depends. The answer, startling as it may seem, might be "no." Maybe spending some time in the political wilderness would be good for Republicans. Or maybe the mere threat of electoral loss will help the GOP find its bearings and change course before it loses entirely the trust of limited-government supporters.

One thing is for sure. A struggle for the heart and soul of the Republican Party is brewing. My hope is that this book will help you understand why.

WHY REAGAN
MATTERS

*How the GOP Became the Party of
Small Government*

A friend of mine named Dave used to be a high school substitute teacher in Phoenix, Arizona, during the late 1990s. One afternoon, he was overseeing a civics class and asked the class to read a few chapters of Barry Goldwater's *The Conscience of a Conservative*. Before the end of class, he asked some students for their reactions. The most interesting response was from the girl who said, "It sounds like this Goldwater guy doesn't like Republicans very much."

Dave told her that the GOP was a very different party in 1962 when Goldwater's book was published. There's a reason why the modern GOP is often called the party of Goldwater and Ronald Reagan and not the party of Nelson Rockefeller and Richard Nixon. This historical perspective is also important for Republicans today: Mimicking the failed Big Government Republicanism of Rockefeller and Nixon is nothing more than, at best, a temporary strategy. Over the long run, it's a recipe for more government.

Even though Goldwater lost the election in a landslide, he won the hearts of conservative voters. His form of fiscal conservatism was influential enough in Republican circles of the late 1960s that even a political chameleon like Richard Nixon had to tack rightward to win the presidential nomination in 1968. But as president, Nixon thoroughly disappointed supporters of limited government.

Nixon mainly believed that it was the role of Republicans to run Big Government better than the Democrats. So he spent taxpayer money *faster* than Lyndon Johnson in many areas—much to the delight of the congressional Democrats. He even created entirely new agencies such as the Environmental Protection Agency and the Occupational Safety and Health Administration, both of which Republicans would later target as the poster-children of a bloated and out-of-control federal government. Nixon, however, took great pride in his creations. In 1972, he built his campaign rhetoric around the fact that government spending had ballooned. Spending on entitlement programs like Social Security and Medicare was kicked into high gear, too, almost doubling in real terms by the time Nixon resigned from office in disgrace.

Nixon's successor, Gerald Ford, further alienated conservatives by nominating as his vice president Nelson Rockefeller, the archrival of Barry Goldwater in 1964. Conservative discontent spurred Ronald Reagan, fresh off two successful terms as California governor, to run against Ford for the 1976 GOP presidential nomination. Reagan was the pick of the burgeoning small-government movement within the party—he was one of the most public supporters of Goldwater and a long-time critic of the big-spending federal politicians—and his campaign signaled the beginning of the end for the Nixon and Rockefeller form of Republicanism. Even though Reagan won a majority of all the votes cast in the GOP primaries that year, Ford won the nomination at that summer's convention. Historians have remarked that the conventioneers' votes belonged to Ford but their hearts belonged to Reagan.[1]

By the time Reagan finally won the presidency in 1980, supporters of limited government had plenty of fresh ideas and the maturity to launch a potentially effective assault on Big Government. By the end of his first year in office, Reagan had succeeded in cutting entire swaths of nondefense programs. And he was also able to slow down the overall growth rate of the total federal budget. During the 1980s, the real yearly growth of all federal spending shrank to 2.6%, down from the 4% average of the previous twenty years. This is one reason Reagan matters.

Looking back at Reagan's rhetoric makes many conservatives yearn for the good old days. There is no doubt that Reagan was the most eloquent spokesman for smaller government in the post-war era. But that's not a sufficient rationale to endow the GOP with the label of the party of small government. The crucial difference between the pre-Reagan GOP and the post-Reagan GOP is the presence of a cadre of small government supporters inside the party. This is another reason Reagan's presidency matters.

By the end of his eight years in office, however, the boundaries of the welfare state were not substantially different than they were when he took the oath of office. This is another reason why the Reagan presidency matters. It showed the limits of the ability and interest of Republicans to cut Big Government even when they are led by someone like Reagan, who made no secret of his belief that government is the problem, not the solution.

Yet Republican strategists and some conservatives today seem to be taking the wrong lessons from the 1980s. They think that since a leader like Reagan couldn't make lasting headway in cutting government, what hope is there for a less eloquent leader? That concern cannot be understated. But just because Reagan's successes weren't as great as some had hoped does not mean that the tangible successes he did achieve should be ignored.

Some conservatives have suggested that it's time to give up trying to scale back government and embrace it instead. Yet, that's exactly the opposite insight that should come from an appraisal of Reagan's presidency. The story of the battle over Reagan's first budget is instructive.

THE WUNDERKIND

At the age of thirty-four, David Stockman became Ronald Reagan's budget director after a four-year stint as a US House representative from Michigan. Journalist William Greider, then a reporter for the *Atlantic Monthly*, described him this way: "His shaggy hair was streaked with gray, and yet he seemed like a gawky collegian, with unstylish glasses and prominent Adam's apple. In the corridors of the Capitol, where all ambitious staff aides scurried about in serious blue suits, Representative Stockman wore the same uniform, and was frequently mistaken for one of them."[2]

William Niskanen, a member of Reagan's Council of Economic Advisors, described the young director of the Office of Management and Budget (OMB) as the *wunderkind* of the White House staff, someone who was "an extraordinary bundle of ideology, energy, and intellect." He had "a remarkable grasp of the details of government programs, in some cases greater than that of the cabinet members whose budget was being reviewed."[3]

To call Stockman a policy wonk might be putting it mildly. He set a very wonky goal for himself upon being named OMB director: memorize the names of up to 1,000 programs and major budget accounts by the time he was sworn in. Stockman had lobbied hard for the OMB job and might have been the first budget director so well prepared for it, too.

Stockman was a bachelor at the time. This freed him up to work fifteen-hour days and seventy-hour weeks. Everyone knew that long hours at the office were necessary if there was even a faint hope that the Reagan budget blitzkrieg would be successful. Stockman often pulled all-nighters.

The most important quality Stockman possessed, however, was that he was a True Believer. He knew by heart and agreed deeply with the intellectual case against the nanny state programs that were created in the 1930s and 1960s. He saw the Reagan presidency as an excellent vehicle to finally return government to its constitutional boundaries. He defended this goal with the zeal of a convert because that's basically what he was. An avowed Marxist while in college during the 1960s, Stockman eventually became an advocate of the free market after striking up a friendship with neoconservative intellectuals like Harvard's James Q. Wilson and Daniel Patrick Moynihan.

The appointment of Stockman was one of the most critical of Reagan's administration. The president even made Stockman an official member of his cabinet. Before then, OMB directors were seen as little more than bureaucratic functionaries. Reagan wanted to push spending cuts to the forefront of the policy

debate, right behind his tax cuts. The elevation of the OMB
director was part of that strategy.[4]

Placing Stockman at the helm of the president's budget-
cutting machine was also a signal. Reagan was showing Congress
that he and his staff were committed and prepared to carry out a
political revolution aimed at scaling back government. He was
challenging the big spenders in Congress to a game of chicken,
and appointing Stockman was the equivalent of tearing the brake
pedal out of the president's car.

RETOOLING THE WHITE HOUSE MACHINE

Reagan came into office with four main fiscal goals: get nondefense spending under control, increase defense spending, cut
income taxes by almost 30%, and balance the budget by 1984.

Everyone in the White House knew this was going to be a
hard sell. Republicans had control of the Senate but only by two
seats. The House—lorded over by uber-liberal Thomas "Tip"
O'Neill of Massachusetts and dominated by the twenty-four-seat
Democratic majority—was readying itself for a bruising fight.
Yet the first battle, as Stockman began to realize, was going to
occur inside the White House.

In the week before the inauguration, the Reagan transition
team issued a set of directives to show that the president was
going to come out slugging against the federal monster. Among
them were an across-the-board hiring freeze, a 15% cutback in
agency travel budgets, and a moratorium on purchasing more
office equipment and furniture.[5] Considering the federal budget
had grown by a total of 17% above inflation under Jimmy

Carter, it was disingenuous for the federal agencies to plead poverty. But they did, and loudly. The squawking was so bad that within a week after Reagan's inauguration Stockman ended up allowing so many exemptions that the directive became virtually meaningless.

It became evident that the Reagan team had to find a way to shift the momentum. They had to combat the tendency of government staffers to defend their budget turf, something that was practically encoded in the cultural DNA of federal agencies.

Even the people whom Reagan had picked to run the major cabinet agencies—many of whom at least agreed publicly with his budget-cutting philosophy—couldn't be trusted to support cuts to their own agencies. Once firmly ensconced in their positions, the career civil servants in the agencies would start to work on the new agency boss and chip away at his commitment to spending discipline. In some cases the staff didn't have very much chipping away to do. Terrell Bell, Reagan's education secretary and the man tasked with carrying out Reagan's goal of eliminating the Department of Education, is a perfect example of one of the poorest appointments Reagan made to a cabinet-level agency. Bell, instead of being a White House ally, turned out to be one of the key opponents to downsizing the federal government's bloated education apparatus. In his memoirs years later he wrote, "Those who accused me of being part of the education establishment were right."[6]

Stockman wrote in his memoirs, that a "'gang-bang' dynamic . . . had already developed among the cabinet."[7] That "gang-bang" dynamic was what threatened to scuttle the budget plan before it had even left the confines of the White House. Normally the director of OMB would send the proposed budget cut plan to the individual cabinet secretaries first. That would usually allow plenty of time for those officials to protest the cuts by running to the president—or the press—using as backup the briefing books prepared for them by staff members opposed to budget cuts. That would lead to newspaper stories denouncing the cuts. Then the overwhelming volume of complaints from lobbyists and activist groups would eventually kill the proposal.

Stockman usually had backup from Reagan on his proposals, and none of them would have gotten very far without support from the president. The main exception was the president's usual deference to Caspar Weinberger, the secretary of defense. A large defense buildup was one of Reagan's top budget goals. Weinberger usually got what he wanted, and this often jeopardized Reagan's other budget goals. Still, Stockman was able to compose a wide-ranging list of cuts in domestic programs. "By early in the week of the 26 January," Stockman writes, "we had the new budget-cutting machine oiled and rolling. When we switched off the ignition eight days later, nearly every vestige of cabinet opposition to budget cuts had been run over. The cuts we'd made included everything from [education aid] to subsidies for [synthetic fuels], physician training, the postal service, Amtrak, local sewer plant construction, and low-income housing, as well as scores of grant programs for community development and health, education and social services."[8]

A list like that might be enough to make someone scratch his head and say, "The federal government funded *that* sort of stuff?" The bad news is that it did. The even worse news is that it still does.

The initial push by the Reaganites to cut the budget did toss opponents back on their heels, a position that supporters of Big Government had not been in for decades. The White House won its initial battles simply by going on the offensive and taking advantage of the element of surprise. In politics as in physics, though, momentum eventually lags after an initial burst of energy if there is nothing to sustain it.

The hardest fights were yet to come.

THE COUNTER-REVOLUTION AND THE MAÑANA SYNDROME

The trial balloons were floating around Washington a week before Reagan's official unveiling of his plan in a speech to Congress on 18 February. The city buzzed with news about proposed cuts to federal activities ranging from arts programs to farm subsidies, school lunches to food stamps. Opposition was quick, loud, and overheated. Leon Shull, national director of the group Americans for Democratic Action, called the budget a "rape of the American middle class and poor people." AFL-CIO leader Lane Kirkland called the Reagan plan an "unnecessary and unwise destruction of social and economic advances of the past 50 years."[9] A coalition of feminist groups issued a press statement suggesting the Reagan budget would "endanger the rights for which woman have struggled over the last several years."[10]

It was the first time in recent memory that any president had presented such a long list of budget reductions. Close to three hundred major programs would receive cuts or orders to cease operations. The total savings accounted for, in 1981 dollars, $49 billion—only about 7% of the total amount the government would spend that year, but a good start nonetheless. Even with these program terminations, total federal spending was still expected to grow by 5.7%, mostly because defense increases out-stripped the declines in nondefense programs. But the rate of overall budget growth was much lower than the rate of inflation that year (10%). Proposing such a budget did take political courage since it cut government spending in inflation-adjusted terms, even if spending was still going up in nominal terms.

However, in 1981 there existed in Washington—then as now—a bizarre assumption about federal spending. That assumption is called "baseline budgeting." It works like this: Imagine Congress expected the budget to grow by 11% in fiscal year 1982, as was estimated in Jimmy Carter's final budget. Instead, Reagan proposed a 6% increase. Most sensible people would ask, "What's the problem? That's still an increase, isn't it?" But Washingtonians don't think that way. Instead of calling this a 6 percentage-point increase, they would call this a 5 percentage-point *cut*. It's mainly a game of redefinition, and the White House was willing to play that game.

As presidential aide Martin Anderson wrote in his memoirs, "The president was not calling for reductions in federal spend-ing, or even for just holding the line. All he wanted to do was stop it from growing so fast. Repeatedly, during the campaign, in the transition, and then at White House meetings, Reagan would look around him and say, 'Federal spending is going up like this,' (raising his arm from the shoulder at a 45-degree angle). 'We have to bring it down here,' (lowering his arm to about a 30-degree angle)."[11] To do that, the Reagan team decided not to trim around the edges of every program. Instead, they decided to redefine what the federal government would do by eliminating things the federal government should not do.

After the initial unveiling of the Reagan plan, the lobbying by cabinet staff and members of Congress to knock this or that program off of the budget-cut list became intense. Stockman later detailed various examples of this "Counter-Revolution." First, there was the scuffle over the Urban Development Action Grant program (UDAG). The program had been started in 1978 by the Carter Administration, and cost taxpayers about $650 million a year. It subsidized downtown hotels, ski resorts, and tennis courts under the auspices of "economic development." This program was on the top of any fiscal conservatives hit list.

Then the Secretary of Housing and Urban Development, Sam Pierce, launched a noisy campaign to save the program. The White House switchboard was deluged with "distress calls" from local Republican mayors and businessmen who just happened to be in the redevelopment and construction business. The small groups who were the direct recipients of the program's largesse were triumphant. Presidential advisor Edwin Meese commanded Stockman to restore the program and told him that appealing the decision to Reagan was a no-go. It was one of the most powerful lessons Stockman learned in those critical first months: "It took some time to sink in that the Counselor of the supposedly most ideologically conservative president of the twentieth century had decided not to touch perhaps the most ideologically offensive and wasteful bit of federal spending on the block."[12]

What was the result? Reagan was all too happy to score some

political points with usually hostile mayors and local government officials by pointing out that his administration had spared the UDAG program. It survived for another nine years before it was finally terminated under Reagan's successor, George H.W. Bush. But that doesn't mean the federal government stopped handing out taxpayer money to revitalize shopping malls or build parking lots after 1990. Congress simply renamed the program and socked it away in another part of the HUD budget.

Before he knew it, Stockman started to become an unwitting accomplice to the Counter-Revolution as well. When his plan to eliminate Job Corps—a program that provided job training to indigent teens—was revealed on Capitol Hill, Stockman received a call from Republican senator Orrin Hatch of Utah with a plea to keep the program. As it turns out, one of the major Job Corps facilities was in Utah.

Job Corps, a creature of Johnson's Great Society, was another prime example of exactly the sort of ridiculous government program that Stockman was keen to abolish. The program cost taxpayers $12,000 for each trainee, which by Stockman's calculations was more than the cost of sending each of them to Harvard for a year in 1981. And there was substantial evidence that the program just didn't work.[13]

That's when Stockman fell prey to what he called the Mañana Syndrome. It's a condition that lulls you into thinking you can spare a government program today and still have the ability and political capital to go after it tomorrow, the next month, or the next year. The $600 million Job Corps program was grazed in the proposed Reagan budget, but it ultimately survived the firing squad. And it did so the next year, too, and the year after that. In fact, the program still exists today and costs taxpayers $1.5 billion dollars. That's close to three times as large as it was in 1981, a 55% increase in inflation-adjusted dollars.

The Counter-Revolution continued to be waged by Republican senators who won numerous victories over the next few months. To gather support for the Reagan budget plan among members of his own party, Stockman had to make concessions on a nuclear reactor project for Senate majority leader Howard Baker of Tennessee, protect tobacco subsidies for Senator Jesse Helms of North Carolina, reverse his cuts to NASA for former astronaut Senator Jack Schmitt of New Mexico, promise the survival of the Rural Electrification Administration—a relic of the New Deal—to Senator Strom Thurmond of South Carolina, and spare crop subsidies for a bushel of farm-state senators.

The victory on farm subsidies was probably the biggest win for the forces of the Counter-Revolution. The result of Stockman's decision to leave farm programs untouched was that Reagan eventually ended up signing a new five-year farm bill that boosted crop payments to new heights. Instead of spending $10 billion over five years as the White House originally proposed, the first farm bill Reagan signed was estimated to cost $60 billion.[14] With the benefit of retrospect and better data, we know the cost to taxpayers of Stockman's surrender was actually $88 billion over five years. And how much do taxpayers fork over to farm programs now? Over the past five years, Congress handed $117 billion of taxpayer money to farmers, most of which goes to large agribusinesses and the wealthiest farmers.

THE HINCKLEY EFFECT AND THE ALAMO

The initial momentum that the White House enjoyed in February began to flag by mid-March. The budget was not as well accepted by the Republican-controlled Senate as the White House hoped. The president's opposition in the Democrat-controlled House was having a field day denouncing the supposedly mean-spirited budget.

Then, on the 30th of March, as Reagan was leaving the Washington Hilton in northwest DC after giving a speech to the Construction Trades Council, John Hinckley fired a series of bullets at the president, one of which ricocheted off the narrow space between the frame and the back-door hinge of the president's limousine and lodged itself less than an inch from Reagan's heart. The nation was stunned. The day after the assassination attempt, the Senate was set to debate the budget. The rhetoric was suddenly more subdued. Reporters noticed a clear contrast with the "bitter, partisan debates that marked earlier consideration of the [Reagan budget]."[15]

The momentum had shifted dramatically. Attempts to restore money to various government programs that were on the chopping block failed resoundingly. In fact, the main challenge to the budget plan the day after the assassination attempt came from a fellow Republican. Senator John Chafee of Rhode Island offered an amendment that would have restored $1 billion in funding to numerous education programs, wasteful urban transit programs, home-heating assistance for the poor (the lion's share of which went to the Northeast and states like Rhode Island), and community health programs.

Under different circumstances, many senators of both parties would be rushing to support these programs. Instead, sixteen Democrats joined Republican supporters of the Reagan plan and killed the Chafee bill, 59 to 41. In the end, the Senate approved the basic framework of the Reagan budget by a margin of 88 to 10. Bear in mind that Republicans held only 53 seats in the Senate.

What happened? The truth is that very few senators—only ten, to be exact—wanted to vote against the budget of a popular president who had just stared down death.

Less than a month later, Reagan walked through the doorway of George Washington University hospital where he had successfully recuperated, and stepped triumphantly into his presidential limo. As the story goes, on his first day back in the Oval Office, even before he had said "Good morning" to his senior staff, he uttered a simple command to the White House foot soldiers who were fighting the budget battle: "No compromises!"[16]

Fresh off a victory on the budget in the Senate, Reagan's staff decided the time was ripe for an address to a joint session of Congress. As veteran journalist Hedrick Smith reported on 28 April, the night of the speech: "With a flair for the dramatic moment, President Reagan sought tonight to provide irresistible momentum for his budget package by capitalizing on what his lieutenants regard as a rare 'second honeymoon' with the American public after the attempt on his life 29 days ago."[17]

Even Tip O'Neill practically rolled over. The day before Reagan's speech, he told the press, "Support the President—that's the concern out there—and Congress can read that. I've been in politics a long time, and I know when to fight and when not to fight."[18] The press reports note that O'Neill sounded dispirited. It was obvious which choice he had made.

By May, Reagan's job approval rating was an impressive 67%.[19] But despite Reagan's popularity, passage of his budget plan could not have happened on its own. There were two congressmen who were critical players in the House: Democrat Phil Gramm of Texas and Republican Delbert Latta of Ohio. Gramm, a lanky former economics professor with a thick Texas twang, was a hard-core fiscal conservative. Latta was also deeply committed to a vision of limited government and, according to Stockman, was one of the only congressmen who never asked the budget chief to spare a project or a pet program for his district.

These two men were the co-sponsors of the main legislative vehicle for the Reagan budget in the House. In May, it looked like the Reagan budget was likely to pass, but victory couldn't be assured. There was some hesitancy among the conservative southern Democrats known as the "Boll Weevils." Because the Democrats held only a twenty-four-vote margin in the House, the balance of power was held by these forty-or-so House members. They were already inclined to vote with the president, but they were worried that Speaker O'Neill would do something to hurt them if they voted against their party, such as take away a committee chairmanship or look down his nose at their next campaign fundraising request. It was going to take some more lobbying of the conservative Democrats to pass the president's plan.

The final compelling push was provided by Gramm himself. The day before the vote on the budget, the Boll Weevils met to discuss whether they should vote for Reagan's plan or the one offered by Jim Jones of Oklahoma, the Democratic head of the House Budget Committee. His plan threw out most of the president's proposals and appealed mainly to the big spenders, yet some Boll Weevils were thinking about voting for it mainly because of O'Neill's likely reprisals. So Gramm stood up and told them it was "time to draw the line in the sand." He said he was going to support the Reagan budget, "even if I'm the only person in the House to vote for it."

Gramm next did something that comes naturally to a Texan: He invoked the Alamo. He said it was clear to him that if William Barrett Travis, commander of the Texas forces at that ill-fated battle, asked for a debate instead of drawing a line in the sand, "there never would have been a battle."

Jack Hightower, also a Texan, reminded Gramm that everyone who crossed the line at the Alamo died, causing many people in the room to nod in agreement. Then Gramm delivered the critical blow. "Yes," said Gramm, "but the ones who didn't cross the line died, too. Only no one remembers their names."[20] The impassioned plea worked. On 7 May, the Reagan budget plan was adopted by a vote of 253 to 176.

The president had worked overtime, too, in an intense lobbying effort to capture the votes of wavering Republicans. To drive the point home, he made a compelling case in a nationally-televised address from the Oval Office. When the votes were counted, all Republicans in the House voted for the bill. The critical swing votes were provided by sixty-three Democrats, most of them conservative southerners like the Boll Weevils.

This was a remarkable outcome, especially when you consider

the invective coming from the supporters of Big Government on the House floor the day of the vote. Ted Weiss of New York called it a "Drop dead, America!" budget. John Conyers of Michigan called it "an economic crime." Thomas Downey of New York even went so far as to say that the budget reductions in the Reagan plan would "kill people."[21]

There is no doubt that the passage of the Gramm-Latta bill was a turning point. There were plenty of concessions made, but the main elements were still intact. However, the bills that passed through the House and the Senate in April and May were simply blueprints. They didn't actually commit the House and Senate to anything. That's one of the little tricks Congress plays. It passes a spending blueprint in the spring—it's called a "budget resolution," and Congress is required to pass one each year. But the resolution is mostly symbolic. It does not have the force of law. In fact, it has the same legal standing as the "sense of the Congress" bills used to make political statements, or the legislation passed each year to authorize the Greater Washington Soap Box Derby. When it comes time to make the actual cuts outlined within the resolution, Congress tends to fudge the numbers, or they simply ignore the blueprint altogether.

It's another example of how the machinery of Congress assists the natural growth of government. And that machinery was about to tear into the Reagan plan.

THE EMPIRE STRIKES BACK

Reagan and his advisors wanted to keep Social Security off the table, but it was hard to avoid talking about it. The program consumed 20% of the federal budget at that time, and keeping it out of the budget equation, along with defense (23% of the budget) and various other entitlement programs that were bargained away in Congress during the debate over the Reagan plan (roughly 17%), left the White House with less than 40% of the budget available for cutting.

But the big problem with Social Security wasn't its cost. The problem was with a demographic bubble looming on the near horizon. Social Security works fine when there are plenty of workers to tax to pay for it all. Once the number of retirees grows faster than the number of workers, you've got a real problem.

There were other structural problems with Social Security that were quite costly, like the provision that let people retire early at age sixty-two. People were living longer than they were in the 1950s when the early retirement option was created. But in 1981 it was just no longer practical.

The biggest structural problem, however, stemmed from the 1970s, when Nixon introduced "wage indexing" of benefits, the "biggest and most costly freebie of all," as Stockman described it. "If you worked for thirty years and productivity growth of the US economy averaged 2% annually over that period, wage indexing threw into the calculation of your pension an extra 2% each year beyond what you had actually paid in taxes (in after-inflation dollars). It was a nice bonus for the millions who got it, but who was going to pay for it? The retirees certainly hadn't."[22] Instead, everyone else was stuck with the bill, and these bills were adding up. The price tag for fifty years of expanded benefits and flagging payroll tax revenue threatened to drive Social Security into a deficit by the summer of 1983.

Stockman came up with a plan to address these provisions by increasing the penalty for early-retirement and cutting in half the annual cost-of-living adjustment (an attempt to remedy the problem of wage indexing), but only for seven years. An alternate, and better, plan floated within the White House at the time would have dealt with the structural problems by actually eliminating wage indexing altogether and raising the retirement age.[23] But Stockman lobbied hard for his plan, and Reagan finally signed off. It was Stockman's belief that getting rid of these unearned benefits and discouraging early retirement would be an easier political fight. Indeed, when looked at in retrospect, the Stockman plan was really very modest. It certainly wasn't the grand sort of reform necessary to fix the program for good.

Even these small reforms sparked a vigorous counter-offensive by the forces of Big Government. Tip O'Neill called the plan "despicable" and a "rotten thing to do." Congressman Claude Pepper of Florida, called it "cruel and insidious."[24] On 20 May, the Senate killed the bill. Not a single senator, Republican or Democrat, voted for it.

The inability and unwillingness to get a handle on Social Security and the other entitlement programs was one of the biggest lost opportunities of the Reagan Revolution. Instead, Reagan ended up endorsing a huge hike in the payroll tax in 1983 in exchange for an increase in the retirement age.

When it came to other entitlement programs such as Medicare—the program to pay for the medical bill of the nation's elderly, which was financed in the same way Social Security was and consequently in the same danger of going bankrupt over time—the White House proposed some minor cost-containment provisions, and some of them were even enacted, but fundamental reform of the program was never seriously considered by the Reagan team. As a result, the price of the program ballooned by 58% even after adjusting for inflation, one of the biggest jumps in any program during the 1980s. In the case of Medicaid—the Great Society program created to pay the medical bills of the nation's indigent—Reagan's innovative proposal to block-grant the programs to states to let them have complete control over it was ignored by Congress.

Later in May, when the House starting getting down to the specifics of the Reagan budget plan, accounting gimmicks abounded. That's how the Senate Agricultural Committee was able to produce legislation that only cut about one-tenth of what it was supposed to cut but made it look like they had hit their target. The House Ways and Means Committee members were able to cook the numbers and make it look as if they had achieved their goals, too. In reality it only turned in half of the real savings required. And so on down the line.

Soon, Stockman had to start cutting deals on lower-priority proposals so the White House had enough votes to claim victory at the end of the day. Once one group of congressmen found out about this, the rest wanted a piece of the action, too. When Stockman met with some northeastern GOP congressmen to hear their demands, his notes from the meeting gave an indication of how much the meeting cost taxpayers: $112 million was restored for Amtrak funding, $400 million for a low-income heating assistance program, $300 million for elementary and special education, and $200 million for youth job training programs.[25]

Before the Senate vote, the White House received a warning

from a senior Republican: "We ain't gonna' make it. Not unless you open up the soup kitchen."[26] Opening the soup kitchen was the tactic of giving money to pet projects of members of Congress to get them to vote your way, and Stockman quickly threw the doors wide open for the senators, too. The madness continued until 26 June when Congress finally passed what remained of the Reagan budget plan.

THE LAST GASP

By most accounts, the 1981 budget was a substantial political win—not that Stockman saw it that way. "The American welfare state emerged from the ordeal largely intact, and from then on the politicians would be in unchallenged control," he later wrote. "The borders of the American welfare state had been redefined, but they had been only slightly and symbolically shrunken from where they had stood before. The half-trillion-dollar per year domestic budget which remained now had incredible staying power, because in surviving the White House assault it had gained renewed political sanction."[27] Reagan advisor William Niskanen comes to a similar but less dramatically-stated conclusion: "The [Reagan] administration never again had the votes to challenge the House Democratic leadership on a major budget issue as it did [in 1981]."[28]

The reception in Congress of the White House's "September Offensive" on spending certainly seems to bear out this conclusion. In an attempt to make up some of the difference between what the president proposed at the beginning of the year and what he eventually got out of Congress, Reagan proposed additional cuts in nondefense spending in September 1981, but even key Republicans balked at it.[29]

Then, with a dramatic flourish, the president shut down the government for a day. On 23 November, Reagan vetoed a congressional resolution to keep the federal government running past the deadline by which Congress was supposed to pass the actual budget. "We're going to cut down, shut down, and eliminate all nonessential government services," Reagan told his advisors. "This is not business as usual. This is not theatrics. It's for real."[30] But the very next day Reagan agreed to a temporary funding measure for the government that contained about half of what he'd asked for in his September request.

In most years thereafter, the White House proposed budgets including almost identical lists of program cuts and terminations to the one the president proposed in 1981. The outcome was the same every year. Congress ignored the list, and Big Government continued to feed.

A LEGACY OF DEBT?

For some, the dark pall that falls over the Reagan legacy is the budget deficits he amassed while in office. Yet the conventional wisdom about the Reagan deficits persists to this day and muddies the discussion of why deficits really matter.

The tax cuts often take center stage in discussions about the deficit. The tax cuts of 1981, which brought income tax rates down by 30% over three years—top marginal rates were 70% in 1981—are considered by many Reaganites as the crown jewel of his presidency. The plan was controversial partly because it seemed to be built on an inherent contradiction. Spending so much on defense and cutting taxes simultaneously would bring the federal government nowhere near balance.

Opponents are quick to point out that Reagan left office with a budget deficit that was twice as large in absolute dollar terms as it was when he took office. But saying the tax cuts caused the deficit is exactly backward. What really drove the deficit to new heights was too much government spending. Consider this: If the federal government had grown by only the rate of inflation in each year of Reagan's presidency, the federal budget would have been balanced in seven years, and he would have left behind a $63 billion surplus.

Taking a look at the macroeconomic environment does not provide much evidence for the critics. The economic recession was pummeling tax collections since before Reagan won the 1980 election. Even if tax rates stayed high, there would still be simply much less economic activity to tax.

There's also another very important historical element to help explain the revenue change: Federal Reserve chairman Paul Volcker's crusade to tame inflation. This was a vital first step to any robust economic recovery—one that Reagan, to his credit, supported completely even in the face of vicious criticism—but it also had the effect of reducing government revenue below expectations. That's because income tax brackets weren't indexed for inflation in 1981. Taxpayers were shuffled into higher tax brackets solely as a result of wages being paid with inflated dollars. This "bracket creep" kept tax receipts higher than they should have been, since the tax code wasn't taxing real income gains but fake ones.

Once inflation started to abate, people began to slide back down the tax bracket scale and tax collections went down, too. According to estimates by government economists, 77% of the increase in the deficit in Reagan's first year in office is a result of the reversal of the bracket creep.[31] You'd be hard pressed to find anyone who would admit that taming inflation was a bad thing, yet much of the revenue decline of the early 1980s was an inevitable side effect of this much-needed policy change.

So what really drove the deficit? Excessive spending. Revenue grew by a total of 20.5% in real terms between fiscal years 1981 and 1989, but spending grew by 23%.

It's not that Reagan or Stockman didn't want to balance the budget. The deficit was a genuine concern of the Reagan administration during both terms. But good intentions alone wouldn't balance the budget. After 1981, Reagan agreed to numerous tax increases. He signed into law bills that had the effect of raising all sorts of revenue in every year of his term except 1988. Unfortunately, these actions didn't bring the budget much closer to balance. Reagan agreed to the taxes because congressional leaders agreed to restrain spending. Congress was supposed to cut three dollars of spending for every one dollar in new taxes. But this was a no-go. Congress broke the bargain, and deficits persisted.[32]

REAGAN, G.H.W. BUSH, AND THE
RISE OF GINGRICH

In the end, Stockman's assessment turned out to be right. Reagan was not able to change the basic outlines of the bloated federal government, and the welfare state remained largely intact. But that does not mean Reagan's presidency was a failure for supporters of limited government.

The portion of the budget increase that is attributable to defense spending is only as controversial as the foreign policies it funded. Reagan viewed the build-up of the US military as an important part of his strategy to defend the nation and topple the Soviet Union. Historians have begun to view the Reagan gambit as an important factor in ending the Cold War. The Soviets couldn't compete much longer with the US in an arms race. The slow failure of the communist system was recognized by Reagan and was central to his decision to increase the defense budget. Some historians have even suggested that the Strategic Defense Initiative missile defense system proposal—often called the "Star Wars" program—helped scare the Soviets into the realization that their days were numbered.[33]

What is undeniable, however, is that the build-up jeopardized fiscal discipline in other areas of the budget. To win support in Congress for Reagan's defense initiatives, he used funding for domestic programs as a bargaining chip.[34] One of the saving graces here, of course, is that Reagan at least tried to offset the increase in the defense budget with cuts elsewhere, even if they were nowhere near enough to balance the budget. At the end of eight years, Reagan had only been able to kill four programs of any substantial cost, and he actually created one new big one: an entire cabinet-level agency for veteran's affairs.[35]

Yet Reagan's first year in office turned out to be the most productive of his entire presidency in terms of scaling back government spending. By the end of his first year, domestic discretionary programs—the budget category that excludes defense and entitlement spending but includes all other federal spending on programs in education, energy, housing, commerce, and transportation—were sliced by a total of $36 billion (inflation-adjusted), amounting to a real cut of about 12.6%. Big Government had clearly been dealt a blow. Even though spending crept up during the rest of Reagan's presidency, it didn't rise by enough to swallow this initial gain. Non-entitlement domestic spending was $27 billion lower in 1989 (in real dollars) when Reagan left office than it was in 1981. It wasn't until 1992—George H.W. Bush's final year in office—that inflation-adjusted spending on these sorts of programs cost taxpayers in the aggregate as much as they did in 1981.

What is also remarkable about Reagan's tenure is that although he wasn't able to permanently scale back the boundaries of the federal government, he *was* able to slow its overall growth. Reagan presided over the smallest inflation-adjusted yearly budget increase of any full-term president since Eisenhower.

Even in the area of entitlement spending—the other major budget category besides defense that was the main contributor to the budget deficit—Reagan applied the brake. The real annual average growth rate under Reagan was the lowest since the Great Society began and still stands today as the slowest growth rate under any post-Johnson presidency.

The federal budget was smaller overall as a share of the economy when Reagan left office, too. It dropped from 22% of GDP to 21%.

Reagan's biggest victory was clearly over domestic programs. The budgets of eight cabinet-level agencies grew slower than the rate of inflation throughout Reagan's eight years in office: Agriculture, Commerce, Education, Energy, Health and Human Services, Labor, Transportation, and the Veteran's Administration. No president of the past forty years has been able to pull that off.

Overall, Reagan's presidency was surprisingly effective at controlling the federal budget, even if it didn't scale it back. Reagan promised to slow down the march of Big Government, and he did. It was a tentative but necessary first step to prove to voters that the GOP was a party of small government. This was not Nixon's GOP anymore.

Another important element was Reagan's consistent and compelling speeches that cast the need to reduce the size and scope of government, not just as a fiscal obligation but as a moral one as well. Big Government, to paraphrase Barry Goldwater, does violence to the Constitution. Smaller government is an end worth pursuing in and of itself. Regan solidified this as Republican gospel.

Nobody expected to scale the federal government back to its constitutional boundaries within one presidency, least of all Reagan himself. This was going to be a generations-long task and would require continued commitment over the next few decades.

But after Reagan handed over the reins, it became obvious that Bush had little interest in shrinking government. This was an important lesson for Republicans in an historical sense. It reminded limited-government conservatives within the party that they had to fight harder for what they really believed and not take for granted that someone who simply calls himself a Republican would share the same goals. In one of those unpredictable twists of history, George H.W. Bush's abandonment of fiscal conservatives was a vital spark to Newt Gingrich's Republican Revolution of 1994.

THE SHORT-LIVED REVOLUTION

Advances and Retreats in the Assault on Big Government

Defeat is an integral part of the lifecycle of ideological movements. Barry Goldwater's electoral defeat didn't kill the small government movement within the Republican Party but instead made it stronger. Fiscal conservatives were mobilized in a way that nobody could have foreseen after the landslide 1964 election of Lyndon Johnson. Without that experience, Reagan's successful presidential run would not have been possible.

The same could be said of the betrayal of the GOP's limited-government principles by Reagan's successor, George H.W. Bush, and his subsequent loss of the presidency. Without it there may never have been a Republican Revolution of 1994.

Bush was not much of an ally to small government conservatives in the first place. When he assumed the presidency, he purged most of the Reaganites from the White House staff and cabinet agencies.[1] Bush's budget philosophy did not resemble that of a small government proponent, either. With the Soviet Union on the ash heap of history and the Cold War effectively over, the need for the large military expenditures of the previous decades disappeared. The decline in the defense budget unlocked what many called the "peace dividend," but this windfall did not make its way back to the wallets of taxpayers or help achieve a

balanced budget. Instead, it mostly fueled a spending binge on
nondefense programs. While real defense spending went *down* by
3.8% annually during Bush's four-year term, non-entitlement
spending went *up* by 3.3%, and entitlement spending went up by
4.8% each year.[2]

For fiscal conservatives, Bush's tax hike was the last straw.
Some analysts even suggest that Bush's abandonment of the fiscal conservative voter base was a critical factor in his loss to Bill
Clinton.[3] If Republicans are going to act like Democrats anyway,
what's the use in showing up to vote for a GOP candidate? When
Republicans lost the White House, it brought the party activists
to a realization that they had to return to the principles of small
government.

The House GOP leader at the time, Bob Michel of Illinois,
was also seen by small government conservatives as part of the
problem. He was a strong supporter of the Bush tax hike and
fought for its passage, against the protests of the more conservative members of Congress. In fact, the leaders of what eventually became known as the Republican Revolution of 1994 led
the congressional insurgency against the Bush tax increase of
1990. Michel's truce with Big Government signaled to those
House conservatives why it was vitally important to overturn the
old guard in Congress.

Bush's loss of the presidency in 1992 opened the door for a
young upstart from Georgia named Newt Gingrich to resurrect
the Reagan message of smaller government and bring it back to
the center of Republican policymaking. When Michel retired,
Gingrich handily won the House minority leader post. Just over
one year later, the GOP won one of the most historic congres-

sional victories in history, built on the overarching principle of restraining the appetites of the federal government.[4]

Gingrich—a former college history instructor—liked to put the Republican Revolution in historical context. He understood the similarities between what he was trying to do and what Reagan tried to do. He envisioned the new GOP congressional majority would presage a cultural revolution in Washington DC. "The real breaking point is when you find yourself having a whole new debate, with new terms. That's more important than legislative achievements," Gingrich told a reporter on the first day of the 104th Congress. "We'll know in six months whether we have accomplished that. Reagan didn't quite pull it off."[5]

Representative Christopher Cox of California—a former senior associate counsel to Reagan who was first elected to Congress in 1988—read David Stockman's memoirs four times. "Revolutions have a very short half-life," Cox said. "If you don't ask for [what you want] early, you won't get it. The window closes on your fingers." Instead of concluding that the Reagan vision was just too radical to survive as a guiding political philosophy, Cox held the opposite opinion. "It didn't go far enough," he explained. Cox was also acutely aware that his fellow members of Congress could easily succumb to the temptation to run Big Government their way, not eliminate chunks of it. "The big risk is that we will seek to use the national government to achieve conservative objectives rather than using our mandate to reduce the size and power of the federal government."[6]

Few people understood the shortcomings of the Reagan years better than Stockman himself, and there were few people with a greater sense of what the new Republican Revolution could do to limit government. At a lunch in DC, with a group of old Reagan staffers who now found they were holding the reins of power in Congress, Stockman urged the attendees to seize the chance to complete what the Gipper started fourteen years before. "Don't let it slip through your fingers," he implored them.[7] The torch had been passed.

THE HUMAN BOTTLE ROCKET
AND THE FRESHMEN

If history repeats itself, it must have recurring character types as well. The David Stockman character of the Republican Revolution—the role of the hard-charging budget cutter—is played by John Kasich of Ohio who, at age forty-two, became chairman of the House Budget Committee upon the GOP takeover of Congress.

Like Stockman, Kasich was widely regarded by all, even his political adversaries, as a deeply principled and energetic advocate for smaller government. Alice Rivlin, Clinton's budget director, called him "fearless."[8] According to the *Washington Post*'s David Maraniss and Michael Weisskopf, "Kasich was anything but the green eyeshade sort, more of a human bottle rocket than a patient numbers nerd, but he had a peculiar attraction to the arcane art of the budget."[9] Gingrich called him "one of the two most brilliant leaders we've got in the House."[10]

Kasich had the task of preparing a budget that eliminated the federal deficit by 2002. To do that, he was going to have to get the House to pass bills that would eliminate hundreds of programs. In many respects, he would have to be even more aggressive than Stockman. Luckily, Kasich had some allies in this battle that Stockman didn't: the 1994 freshmen Republican class.

It's important to view how unique the 1994 electoral victory was in terms of who it brought to Congress. Republicans held 230 seats in the House in 1995, so they now had a majority plus twelve votes if every Republican voted the party line. But not all Republicans would. That's why the freshmen mattered. There were seventy-three brand new members of the House, close to a full third of the entire Republican majority. They held the balance of power. The battles against Big Government were not going to be won simply because there were more Republicans in Congress. The battles would be won because there was more of the sort of Republican committed to making government smaller.

Most of the freshmen weren't partisan drones. Many were passionately committed to taming the federal behemoth and were willing to vote against the GOP leaders if they sold out the cause of limited government. As Lindsey Graham of South Carolina—elected first to the House in 1994 and now a senator—put it, "We have been the conscience of the election. When our leadership gets back in the politics-as-usual mode, we need to say, whoa, wait a minute; that's not why we got elected."[11] They saw themselves as emissaries sent temporarily by the voters to Washington on a specific mission: to tame Big Government.

Half of the freshmen had never held even local elective office before.[12] Over half of the freshmen class was younger than 45 years old.[13] Many of them were businessmen before coming to Congress and weren't looking for a new career path. Some were even willing to go so far as to limit themselves to a fixed number of terms in office to prove the seriousness of their intent not to let Washington corrupt their principles. Some even kept that promise.

Sam Brownback of Kansas, now a US senator, was one of the very few House freshmen who did not sign the Contract with America, but his description of what the 1994 election was really about was shared by most who did sign the Contract: "Many of us ran a very aggressive, very ideological campaign. I ran a very conservative campaign, saying we should reduce the size of the federal government, reform the Congress, and return to the basic values that built this country."[14]

The election of 1994 was a populist election like the elections of the 1890s, suggested Brownback, but with Big Government as the target of voter anger, not the railroads and banks. "Most of my colleagues are very ideologically driven," he said. "A number of us are the political children of Ronald Reagan. We came of political age under Ronald Reagan. We could say, This is someone I can believe in, he has a core set of principles."[15]

Upon arriving in Washington, the House freshmen were treated to an orientation that brought them up to speed on all sorts of congressional procedures and public policy topics. It was there that they began to realize their power to actually affect change.

At the retreat, about thirty freshmen, including Brownback, Graham, John Shadegg of Arizona, and Joe Scarborough of Florida, met in the lobby of the hotel they were staying at, began to chat, and an idea soon percolated. They knew that part of the problem with Congress was the entrenched power that the chairmen of the individual committees had for as long as they held office—and with incumbent reelection rates north of 90%, that could be a lifetime. Why not term-limit committee chairmen? That would hinder the ability of future chairmen to build their fiefdoms and forbid them from lording over them indefinitely. And, by that logic, why not term-limit the Speaker of the House, too?

Because the freshmen still didn't know each other that well at this point, they didn't realize that some reporters were milling among them at this meeting. When those reporters broke the story of the term-limit plan, it ended up on the pages of a newspaper that eventually found its way to Newt Gingrich's desk. But instead of resisting the idea, he embraced it. So, on the first day the House was in session, it approved a term limit of eight years for the Speaker of the House and six years for committee chairmen, a limit that still stands today.[16]

On budget issues, the freshmen found a kindred spirit in John Kasich. He joined the twenty-member caucus they formed called the New Federalists—a group designed to hold together a block of crucial votes that would provide backbone in case the GOP leadership went soft on the budget. He even attended their press conference on a policy proposal that was at the heart of the budget-cutting agenda: a plan to eliminate three entire cabinet agencies—the Departments of Commerce, Education, and Energy.[17]

These three agencies were long-time targets of fiscal conservatives and had absolutely no basis in the Constitution and were clearly the most unjustifiable agencies in the entire federal budget. The Department of Commerce was the home for all sorts of corporate welfare programs that subsidized private businesses. The Department of Education was one of Jimmy Carter's creatures, designed to expand the unwarranted role of the federal government in education and an agency that survived Ronald Reagan's pledge to eliminate it. The Department of Energy was another Carter creation and the textbook example of an agency that should be abolished because its only practical purpose was to meddle in the free market, usually with disastrous results.

Kasich's aggressive budget plan included eliminating these three agencies and close to 300 individual programs, like the Corporation for Public Broadcasting, the Travel and Tourism Administration, worker training programs, wasteful urban housing bureaucracies, and corporate welfare programs like the Advanced Technology Program (a source of subsidies to high-tech companies), the Economic Development Administration, and the International Trade Administration. In fact, many of these programs were on David Stockman's list of terminations fourteen years before.

Kasich knew keeping the plan intact through the rest of the year would be a tough fight because of opposition from entrenched interests on K Street, where the offices of the highest-paid and biggest-caliber lobbyists were located. "It will be very difficult, because of the 'Zorro Principle'—death by one thousand cuts," explained Kasich. "People affected by a government program will be very vocal that the program be maintained—they'll organize in members' districts and say why that member must vote to continue the program."

Some of the staunchest supporters of programs that were the most odious to fiscal conservatives—particularly agricultural programs and business subsidy programs—were Kasich's partisan brethren. Even support for the National Endowment for the Arts was quite strong in the GOP. As Kasich pointed out, "We have a lot of rich Republicans. Support of the arts is thought of as a Democratic deal, but it's Republican."[18]

Kasich's first test came in the months leading up to the vote on the spending blueprint. By 2 May, Kasich had unanimous approval from Republicans on the Budget Committee of the plan he had crafted. Over the next few days, he presented the plan to the House members gathered at a GOP strategic retreat in Leesburg, Virginia. The problems began with Pat Roberts of Kansas, a seven-term congressman and head of the House Agricultural Committee. He haggled with the budget chairman to restore a large share of the money cut from farm programs, and Kasich eventually agreed to settle for just over half of what he had originally proposed.

The powerful Transportation and Infrastructure Committee chairman, Bud Shuster of Pennsylvania, lambasted Kasich's proposed privatization of Amtrak and freeze on mass transit projects, so Kasich relented on those programs, too.[19] By the end of the year, transportation would turn out to be one of the areas in which Republicans delivered the smallest cuts.

The Zorro Principle came close to prevailing, but in the end Kasich won much of what he was fighting for. The House budget resolution still ended up looking like something fiscal conservatives thought they'd only see in their wildest dreams. It included the elimination of the Departments of Energy, Education, and Commerce, and the termination of almost 300 programs. It cut all sorts of other government programs without relying on the tired and disingenuous gimmick of merely reducing the rate of growth and calling it a cut. These were real cuts to foreign aid programs, farm subsidies, environmental programs, and community development boondoggles. Defense even took a small hit in the form of a 1.5% decrease from the previous year's level. Kasich's plan was actually more aggressive than the Stockman plan of 1981.

The House Democrats weren't able to mount much of an opposition. The plan offered by minority leader Richard Gephardt got clobbered. Only 100 members of the House supported it. In fact, more Democrats voted against it than for it. The Republican budget resolution passed the House by a 55% majority.[20] Bear in mind that the GOP only held 53% of all House seats.

Now it was the Senate's turn to produce a similar plan. There was already a distrust of the Senate by conservatives in the House, and the weak plan that the Senate finally presented only fueled more suspicion in the ranks. The presidential aspirations of majority leader Bob Dole were widely known, and there was a sense by some in the House that he was not truly committed to smaller government.

Conservatives did have some allies in the Senate, particularly veteran budget-cutter Phil Gramm. A Republican since entering the Senate in 1984, Gramm held a seat on the Senate Budget Committee, and throughout the next year he would be a key source of pressure on the Senate to get a handle on spending. "The glue that holds the Contract with America together is cutting government spending," Gramm said on the opening day of the 104th Congress.[21]

Yet, there was already ample opposition from some of the Senate's old-guard members. Kasich's counterpart in the upper chamber, Senate Budget Committee chairman Pete Domenici, strongly opposed abolishing the Department of Education and Energy, for instance.[22] And the budget resolution that passed out of the Senate only eliminated 100 government programs, while even President Clinton's budget eliminated 130.[23]

Once the differences between the House and Senate versions were ironed out, the only cabinet agency targeted for elimination was the Department of Commerce. But many of the other proposed cuts were still intact. The plan passed the House by a vote of 239 to 194. The Republicans were joined by eight Democrats, some of them members of the fiscally conservative "Blue Dog" caucus, the 1990s version of the Boll Weevils. In the Senate, the plan passed on a strict party-line vote with every Republican voting for it, even the big spenders like Chafee of Rhode Island and Olympia Snowe of Maine.[24]

Republican leaders were overjoyed. Gingrich told reporters: "After decades of reckless spending, we are committed to making government leaner, more efficient and cost-effective."[25] After the vote, Kasich was giddy. "This is why we came to Congress," he professed.[26]

Now that Gingrich and Kasich had gotten the House to agree to a nonbinding resolution, it was Kasich's job to get the majority to actually cut these programs. Time was of the essence. "If we don't balance the budget this term, it's over. I think people are willing to sacrifice a bit now," he said.[27] The freshmen would play a key role, too. The main reason any of the budget cuts remained intact at all was because of the twenty-member New

Federalists coalition, the ranks of which would grow to thirty congressmen over the next twelve months.

CUTS FOR THEE, BUT NOT FOR ME

The trouble began that summer when the appropriations bills began to roll through Congress. One of the first battles was over the Appalachian Regional Commission (ARC). Created in 1965 by Lyndon Johnson, the program cost taxpayers $164 million in 1995 and funded economic development assistance to just thirteen states from New York to Tennessee, Alabama, and Mississippi. The phrase "economic development assistance" is Washington-speak for money going to contractors and pork-barrel projects.

Even though the ARC was eliminated in the Kasich budget plan, it was given new life by the House Appropriations Committee. Three-term congressman Scott Klug of Wisconsin sponsored an amendment that would eliminate ARC altogether. During the debate over the amendment, Klug cited various projects of questionable value, like a $750,000 grant to build a new football stadium for the Carolina Panthers, an access road for a Pennsylvania ski resort, and grants to the Alabama Music Hall of Fame. Thirty freshmen voted for Klug's proposal, but it wasn't enough to stop the onslaught from supporters of the program. The amendment was defeated by a close to three-to-one margin.[28] Today the ARC still exists, and although it costs taxpayers a fraction of what it used to—$74 million—it serves as a reminder of what would become the GOP's eventual inability to change the general outlines of the federal government.

Klug's next amendment to eliminate the Tennessee Valley

Authority (TVA), after the Appropriations Committee salvaged it, met a similar fate, too. Conservatives since Barry Goldwater had hoped to eliminate or privatize this government-owned electricity company. As the budget cutters would point out, the Tennessee valley has had sufficient electricity for decades and most of it was provided by private electric companies. Besides, since its inception during the New Deal era, the TVA took on new roles and expanded its empire—and, therefore, the ability to get a larger budget each year. Now the TVA was also in the business of managing public land, maintaining navigation facilities and docks, and funding a variety of so-called economic development projects.

"This is pure pork," argued Klug. "How can we justify federal tax dollars . . . going to such functions as boat landings, campgrounds, and logger education?" But when given the chance to finally put an end to such an unnecessary and bloated government program, many House Republicans rallied to its defense. The amendment died but by the less lopsided margin of 284 to 144. Forty-two freshmen voted to kill the TVA.[29]

A pattern was emerging. Programs that had sufficient parochial support among some GOP politicians were saved, and those that didn't ended up on the cut list. The programs that tended to have more Republican support were those that dispensed subsidies to private businesses, often called corporate welfare. Take the Market Promotion Program (MPP), for example, a federal program that gives matching funds to US companies to advertise their products overseas. Over the previous ten years taxpayers footed the bill for $1.25 billion in international ad campaigns for companies like Pillsbury, McDonald's, Sunkist,

and the Ernest and Julio Gallo vineyards. Donations from many
of the corporate and agricultural interests that benefited from the
program could be found in the reelection coffers of many farm-
state congressmen, including some of the freshmen. Call it the
symbiosis of Big Business and Big Government.

When a bipartisan amendment to the agriculture funding
bill was presented to eliminate the MPP, some of the conservatives championed it. Matt Salmon of Arizona, one of the freshman budget hawks, called on his House colleagues to end welfare
for, "Ronald McDonald, the Keebler elves, the dancing raisins,
and the Pillsbury Doughboy."[30] Salmon's pleas were to no avail.
The amendment went down to defeat with the freshmen class
almost evenly split. The factor that was the best predictor of how
a particular House member voted was whether he or she represented a farm state.

The MPP survived and eventually grew 5% by 1996.[31] The
program evolved, too, becoming harder to cut with each subsequent attempt. Its name was changed to the innocuous-sound-
ing Market Access Program, and its subsidies were redirected to
trade associations. That the money now went to the associations
and not a specific company, however, is hardly a consolation.
The subsidies still tend to benefit the largest corporations
within those industries. Today the federal government spends
over $100 million each year on this and other "market access"
activities.

The story was the same throughout the summer, and the corporate welfare state survived the Republican Revolution mostly
intact. It wasn't that budget cutters in Congress lacked for targets:
There were at least 125 corporate welfare programs costing tax-

payers at least $75 billion in 1995. Kasich's budget did eliminate or slice deeply many of them.[32] There even seemed to be a political consensus that it was time to end these egregious subsidies. When *Business Week* magazine took a poll of top executives, it found more than half agreeing with the notion that corporate welfare was bad, and even two-thirds agreed with scrapping the Department of Commerce.[33]

Yet only five major corporate welfare programs met their demise. Among them was the Interstate Commerce Commission—cost: $15 million—an agency that mostly served the interests of trucking and railroad companies by keeping competitors out. Even President Clinton recommended it for termination. Most of the corporate welfare programs that did face the ax, however, were tiny, like the $2 million subsidy to the US Mink Export Development Council for the fashion shows it sponsors abroad.[34]

Looking at the budgets of the top targets on Kasich's cut list—the corporate welfare programs of the Department of Commerce and Energy, the TVA, the ARC, farm subsidies, and the export promotion subsidies of the Department of Agriculture—you find there was at least $14.6 billion ripe for cuts in the summer of 1995. In the end, those programs were only nicked by a total of $1 billion.[35] The biggest cuts were to energy subsidies and the TVA, but those were mostly offset by the increases in the other programs, particularly those that resided in the Department of Commerce.

There were good tactical reasons for Republicans to go after corporate welfare, too. By doing so they could have neutralized the criticism that they were simply interested in cutting programs for the poor and not the wealthy. Instead most Republicans preferred a strategy that was geared mainly to bearing down on the programs that their political opponents favored. Those Big Government programs *did* need to be cut, of course, as they compose a much larger share of the federal budget. But the failure to put a spike through the heart of corporate subsidy programs is perhaps one of the biggest missed opportunities of the Republican Revolution. By the end of Clinton's second term, corporate welfare programs cost taxpayers $87 billion, a 14% increase from 1995.[36]

THE CARDINALS RULE

The most coveted committee assignment in Congress is a spot on the Appropriations Committee. It is considered so prestigious and powerful that in the vernacular of Capitol Hill the committee members are called the "Cardinals." Like the cardinals of the Roman Catholic Church, these princes of the purse-strings are held in awe and respect. Sometimes they are feared. The Cardinals usually control who gets what pork project or who gets their favored provision into a must-pass piece of legislation. They can make your political life heaven or hell. Their job is to spend taxpayer money, not save it. When Republicans were in the minority, the Cardinals were seen as the drivers of the Big Government growth machine. Now that the Republicans were in the majority, the guys at the controls would end up acting a lot like the ones they replaced.

Gingrich knew at the beginning it would be necessary to tame the Cardinals, and he wanted to put someone at the head of the committee he thought wouldn't bat an eyelash at cutting the budget. Gingrich endowed Bob Livingston of Louisiana—someone he thought was more ideologically pure than the others on the committee—with the chairmanship. Gingrich even passed over three committee members with more seniority to give Livingston the top spot on Appropriations, something that was unheard of before 1995.

In February, the Speaker of the House met with the new chairman and the rest of the Cardinals and told them that budget cuts were at the forefront of the revolution and he needed their help. Asking an appropriator to yield to the pressures of spending discipline is a bit like asking a junkie to give up his narcotic. But Gingrich was confident the new chairman could be trusted to keep the Cardinals in line.

Yet when it came time to eliminate the Department of Commerce, the Cardinals refused to do it. When asked about that year's agenda for the committee, Livingston noted, "We never said we'd close departments."[37] The freshmen were enraged. It was a harsh lesson in how difficult it would be to break the iron triangle of the special interest groups, the Cardinals, and the Appropriations subcommittees. As Sam Brownback noted, the budget process "was built to build, and then when you want to get rid of something, it's built to protect."[38]

The members of the New Federalists were looking to Gingrich for any signs that he would help them eliminate the department, or they might just withhold their support for critical bills later on, something that could make his leadership look weak. So Gingrich persuaded William Klinger, head of the Government Reform and Oversight Committee, to include the department's elimination in a larger piece of legislation later in the fall.[39] But when that bill finally reached the president's desk, Clinton vetoed it. Thus the battle to terminate the Department of Commerce ended with a whimper. The Republican leadership never again attempted to dismantle the agency, and one of the prime goals of the Republican Revolution was dashed for good.

Other House leaders had problems with the appropriators, too. Majority whip Tom DeLay of Texas, the third-in-command of the House leadership, tried to kill a puny $1 million Advisory Council on Historic Preservation, but the Appropriations Committee defeated his plan handily. "If we can't eliminate this, we can't eliminate anything," a disgruntled DeLay told the press.[40]

Meanwhile, Kasich was having his own troubles with the Cardinals. When Kasich tried to de-fund the Overseas Private Investment Corporation—another corporate welfare program that provides cut-rate loans to corporations investing abroad—Livingston led the charge to preserve it. In fact, the chairman went one step further and won a vote to increase OPIC's budget.[41] When Kasich tried to go after export subsidies, Livingston took to the floor to defend that program, too, and scored another win for Big Government.[42]

When asked by a reporter about the scuffles between him and Kasich, Livingston expressed little interest in paying much heed to the budget chairman's list of cuts. "He can run his business, and I'll run mine," he said.[43] An exasperated Kasich told a journalist that perhaps the budget-cutters might need another election to replace the old guard with folks who were more zealous about reducing spending.[44]

Kasich also had opposition from the House leaders when he tried to de-fund the $15.3 billion purchase of twenty more B-2 "Stealth" bombers. The Pentagon already had twenty, and they made it very clear they didn't want any more. But Kasich soon found himself butting heads with Bob Livingston and Tom DeLay. The majority whip fought hard for the aircraft purchase and even worked with lobbyists from Northrop Grumman—the plane's manufacturer—to send out reminders to key congressmen about how many job losses would result in their districts if the B-2 project was ended. It employed a surprising number of people in numerous towns and cities. That's because locating manufacturing plants for all sorts of vehicle parts in multiple key congressional districts is a tried-and-true ploy by defense contractors to maintain support for the continued purchase of their products by the government. With the Air Force brass on Kasich's side, none of the bomber supporters even tried to claim the B-2 was a strategically necessary aircraft. Instead House members were persuaded to view it as just another federal jobs program.

Kasich had seen it all before, of course. He had fought the same battle in most of the previous six years and was even successful a few times in terminating the bomber, only to watch it reappear in Senate legislation and survive. "What's the difference between the B-2 and Dracula?" Kasich used to joke. "Even if you put a stake through the heart of the B-2, it won't die." This time was no different. Even with thirty freshmen allies voting with the budget chief, the stake narrowly missed the heart of the B-2. The proposal failed by three votes. Kasich had been defeated by the leaders of his own party.[45]

When the Cardinals passed on immediately terminating the

National Endowment for the Arts (NEA) and opted instead to phase-down the budget over three years, the freshmen launched a stealth campaign to get the House leadership to deal with the uncooperative appropriators. The budget hawks knew that a phase-down over time was meaningless. It was simply a trick to make it look like Congress would take action in the future, when in reality they would conveniently forget to make the budget cut three years from now. "We don't want to take a lawn mower and run it across the weeds, we have to pull some of [the programs] out by their roots," said Kasich. "The National Endowment for the Arts would not care if we cut their budget by 99%. They know if they get $1 and survive, they'll be back."[46]

The ring leaders of the stealth campaign to get the Republican leaders to talk turkey were two rock-ribbed fiscal conservatives from Oklahoma: former Seattle Seahawks wide-receiver turned congressman Steve Largent, and obstetrician Tom Coburn of Oklahoma, one of the freshmen who had term-limited himself and preferred the moniker "doctor" to "congressman." Joining them were David McIntosh and Mark Souder of Indiana and fellow New Federalists members Sam Brownback, Mark Sanford, Joe Scarborough, and John Shadegg.

On 12 July, the cadre aimed for one of its first victories. They were trying not to tip their hand too early. To avoid arousing any suspicion, they didn't even sit near each other that morning on the floor of the House. It finally came time for a routine proce-dural vote to put the NEA phase-down on the House floor for debate. The New Federalists and their sympathizers had agreed ahead of time to vote against it. By being the key swing votes, they hoped to deal one of the first blows to the House leadership. Sure enough, when the votes were counted, thirty-six freshmen were joined by a handful of Democrats who were less concerned about the content of the bill and more interested in making the GOP leaders look bad. It was enough to tank the legislation.

The Republican leaders went berserk.

Gingrich met with the freshmen and immediately worked out a compromise: a phase-out of the NEA in two years instead of three. The freshmen figured it was probably the best they could hope for under the circumstances and agreed to the deal.[47] So the NEA survived, but with a 22% cut the next year. It was the first time the freshmen were able to flex their muscles, and it sent a strong signal to the House leaders. But in retrospect we can see that the fear of the budget hawks was well-founded. The program didn't really disappear after two or even three years. The NEA still exists today with a $124 million budget, only 43% smaller in real terms than it was when the Republicans took over.

The same thing happened with the Legal Services Corporation (LSC), a program created by Nixon to provide tax-payer-financed legal counsel to welfare recipients. That was the idea, anyway. In practice, much of the money ended up funding political activism aimed at expanding government welfare programs. When the Cardinals declined to kill the program, the cadre of budget hawks threatened another defeat of a routine procedural vote.[48] When the House leaders offered them a 40% cut in the LSC's 1996 budget and a two-year phase-out, the freshmen took that deal, too. But the LSC also survived the two-year expiration date. Its budget is only 34% smaller today in real terms than it was in 1995. In other words, both the LSC and the NEA were able to escape termination while also keeping more than half the budget they had before the Republicans took control.

Another problem the budget cutters faced was the Senate. Every time the House would forward a bill to cut spending, the Senate would just lump some of the money right back in and salvage programs that Kasich wanted to send to the junk heap. When the two bills were reconciled, the Senate usually got what it wanted. In the aggregate, however, what John Kasich was worried about—that the Senate and the House Cardinals would restore a few million dollars here and there and before you knew it the budget was as big as before—had not entirely doomed the Republican plan yet. Although the big cuts were to come, the bills finally signed into law by the president did mandate actual cuts of $3 billion in discretionary spending, amounting to a 5% decrease when compared to the previous year's budget. One-third of that came from eliminating fifty-seven programs.

The last big piece of legislation on which the fiscal conservatives could pin their hopes was the bill to fund the Departments of Labor, Health and Human Services, and Education. It's one of the biggest bills Congress tackles every year. It was in this legislation that over half of the program terminations in the Kasich plan were to occur. The list included among its highest-profile targets some federal job training programs, "community development" boondoggles, and the Low Income Home Energy Assistance Program, through which the federal government helped pay the utility bills of the poor.

Also on Kasich's hit list was Goals 2000, the federal education program started by George H.W. Bush that had become a pet project of the Clinton administration. The program created a slew of new bureaucracies and was another example of the federal government's attempt to slowly hijack a fundamentally state and local function. Yet, fiscal conservatives took eliminating federal education programs as an article of faith. The federal government just simply had no business butting its head into the classrooms of kindergarten all the way through twelfth grade. Typical of the traditional conservative view of the Department of Education were the sentiments of Chester E. Finn, former assistant secretary of education in the Reagan administration. "It is a meddlesome, bullying force," said Finn. "It impedes more reform than it fosters."[49] Close to a third of all the programs on the House termination list were located in the Department of Education.[50]

The fight was a close one: the Labor-HHS-Education bill only passed by eleven votes in the House, with all Republicans except eighteen voting for it.[51] The program terminations remained largely intact and would amount to a cut of $7 billion (or 10%) from the previous year's spending levels. It was seen as a remarkable achievement to keep most of the GOP team together for the vote, and it wouldn't have been possible without a push by Kasich and Gingrich to round up support.

But the victory was short-lived. Once the bill made its way to the Senate, it got bogged down in arguments over which programs should receive more money, not less, and most of the savings in the bill began to evaporate almost instantly. Even the Senate's watered-down version would have spurred a Clinton veto, but it never got that far.

Congress was already a month past the deadline for passing a budget for the year. So the Republicans sent a "continuing resolution" to the president to keep the government operating while they and the White House worked out an agreement over the rest of the appropriations bills. Clinton promptly vetoed the bill, and the federal government shut down on 13 November. The shutdown lasted six days. When the government reopened, GOP leaders thought a deal with Clinton was just around the corner. Then budget talks broke down again in December, spurring another shutdown.

This one lasted two weeks—the longest shutdown in US history.

SHOWDOWN

During the negotiations between the president and the Republicans, many of the arguments raged around the arcana of the budget process—what baseline to track, which economic estimates should be followed, and what data should be used to determine whether the plan would actually balance the budget. But whether the budget balanced in seven years (as the GOP wanted) or ten (as Clinton wanted) is immaterial. As should be obvious by now, any future promise of a spending cut is usually never worth the taxpayer-financed paper it's printed on. And estimating future government revenue is a notoriously inexact science, if it can be called a science at all. What really mattered was the line in the sand that the Republicans drew at attempting to balance the budget by cutting spending and not raising taxes. That's not the kind of crusade that George H.W. Bush embarked upon in 1990. And it's not the sort of discussion that would have occurred without a GOP congressional majority ready for a showdown with Clinton over the proper size of government.

But the House conservatives were concerned about what was going on in the closed-door negotiations. They began to fear that their leaders were going to bargain away the gains the Republicans had already made. They were particularly worried about Bob Dole and the Senate. On the feeling of conservative unease, John Boehner of Ohio—Republican conference chairman, a mid-level leadership post—said that while some House members were concerned about the White House's maneuvering, "our greater concern was the Senate. They wanted to balance the budget, but being loved was more important to them. They wanted to do what they'd done all these years—cut a deal."[52]

The House conservatives knew that refusing to open the government was the only way they could get Clinton to move further in their direction. And despite the conventional wisdom at the time, many congressmen noted they were not getting much negative feedback from their constituents.[53] Journalists who followed the events closely admit that Republicans were gaining more traction the longer the government was closed. As Elizabeth Drew of the *Washington Post* wrote in her book about the first year of the 104th Congress, "Clinton had already moved quite a bit [during the shutdown] toward the Republicans, and was prepared to move further."[54]

The worst fears of the conservatives were confirmed when Bob Dole took to the floor of the Senate in January 1996 to put an end to it all by proclaiming, "Enough is enough!" Even Gingrich seemed eager to end the shutdown. When seventeen House Republicans—twelve of them freshmen, including Largent, Souder, and Shadegg—voted against opening the government, Gingrich was enraged and cancelled fundraisers in some of their districts.[55] In the end, a budget deal was finally struck, but only after Gingrich and the Senate negotiators gave Clinton the $5 billion he wanted restored to the budgets of various health, education, job training, and environmental programs.[56]

After the ink had dried on the deal, many pundits suggested that all the Republicans had to show for their efforts was a political black-eye. In retrospect, some observers aren't so sure. Bob Walker of Pennsylvania, one of Gingrich's closest allies, told reporter Major Garrett of Fox News in 2005, "Did we lose an election as a result of it? No. Is there anything really bad that happened congressionally because of the fact that we shut the government down, really? No."[57]

After looking at the election results of the 1996 congressional election—in which the GOP lost a net four seats in the House—National Public Radio's Linda Killian concluded that election can't be seen as a repudiation of the 1994 election. The dozen freshmen who lost did so for the same reason that most politicians lose elections—they were not particularly effective candidates.

Looking at the freshmen who fought the hardest to cut spending, you'll notice that most of them increased their share of the popular vote in 1996. This is remarkable considering the labor unions spent $35 million trying to unseat many of the GOP reformers. That Republicans did so well was also remarkable in light of Clinton's substantial reelection victory. For instance, Tom Coburn, one of the most committed budget cutters, won by 10 percentage points in a district that went for Clinton by seven points.[58] It seems the attempt to cut spending and the eventual government shutdowns didn't hurt the electoral prospects of many of the House members. It might have actually helped.

POSTMORTEM

The government reopened in January 1996, and less than twenty days later President Bill Clinton delivered his State of the Union address. In that speech he uttered the words that sent the GOP into ecstatic applause: "The era of big government is over." Just to make everyone sure they had actually heard him correctly, Clinton uttered the phrase a second time toward the end of his speech. In the eyes of Republicans, it was a seven-word validation of what Gingrich and company had hoped to accomplish: a shift in the terms of the debate in Washington DC away from a presumption that government could solve all problems to one that assumed government was at least part of the problem.

Republicans did accomplish more than just getting Bill Clinton to publicly rebuke the big spenders. In inflation-adjusted terms, the nondefense discretionary budget fell by 4%, marking the first time nondefense spending had been cut since Reagan. It wasn't as much as Kasich had originally proposed (a 5% overall cut in nondefense spending), so by the GOP's own benchmark of success, they fell short. But considering the president was proposing far smaller decreases—and Clinton hadn't even proposed those cuts until he was forced to do so during the government shutdown—this was a genuine achievement.

On the other hand, the Republican Revolution failed to fundamentally reform the biggest entitlement programs—in particular, Medicare, the program that subsidizes medical care for seniors.

Republicans did propose a modest plan to restrain Medicare spending over a seven-year period. Their plan set the rate of real growth at 4% as compared to the anticipated 9% that would have occurred in the absence of cost-containment legislation. Then Clinton and the Democrats mounted a "Mediscare" campaign, alleging that this was a "cut" in Medicare even though the program would still grow substantially.[59] It threw the GOP off their game, and soon the Republicans retreated. Clinton's plan would have also "cut" Medicare spending, since it included an assumption of 5% real annual growth. But the forces of Big Government were obviously uneager to point that out.

Neither the Republican nor the Clinton Medicare proposals, however, made any attempt to fix the structural problems with the program. Because Medicare relies on the same pay-as-you-go financing scheme that Social Security does, the impending mass retirement of the Baby Boomers will make the costs to taxpayers explode in the very near future and threaten to soak future workers with huge tax increases. Cost-containment measures only tinker around the edges and, although useful in the short term, don't do much to change the long-term outlook or change tracks to avoid the impending demographic train wreck. Even when Clinton and the Republicans struck a budget deal in 1997 that included caps on Medicare spending, the agreement didn't do much to shore up the long-term insolvency of the program. They even abandoned a few proposals that would have done some good, such as increasing the age of eligibility for Medicare recipients.[60]

Yet Republicans weren't completely AWOL on significant reforms of other entitlement programs. The biggest long-standing victory came in 1996 with welfare reform. The reform was remarkable enough in that it occurred in an election year. That it occurred with a Democrat in the White House was even more remarkable and would have been practically unfathomable before the Republican Revolution.

The centerpiece of the reform was devolving control over the program to states and placing a lifetime limit on the length of time someone could receive cash assistance. It had all the hallmarks of conservative reform. It ended welfare as an "entitlement" by turning the program into a block grant to be given directly to states. No longer would the operative assumption of the program be that spending would go up automatically based on the size of the welfare rolls. The block grant would be frozen at a specific level and would provide an incentive to states to be innovative and cost-effective in how they administer the program and get welfare recipients into jobs, another primary aim of the reform.

The reform hinged on another core principle held by supporters of smaller government: respect for the individual. The reformed assistance program was no longer based on the assumption that the poor were victims of a larger macroeconomic or racial dynamic that sapped their ability to get a job, but instead was based on the premise that anyone can become productive members of the workforce if given the chance and the incentive.

Ten years later the number of people on welfare is lower than ever before. The unemployment rate among the poor has declined—particularly in those states with more substantial work requirements—and the well-being of the vast majority of former welfare recipients has been generally increased. By most measurements, welfare reform has been a success. It's not likely that this reform could have occurred in the absence of the Republican Revolution.[61] Indeed, in terms of reducing the reach of Big Government, it was a grander achievement than even Reagan was able to muster.

Another legislative achievement was an attempt to wean farmers off federal largesse. That occurred in the form of the Freedom to Farm Act of 1996. Agricultural policy was one of the last remnants of the command-and-control paradigm of New Deal liberalism. Taxpayers were forced to subsidize farmers if the actual price of a chosen crop went below a government-set target price. And, because the government was also hoping to bar against overproduction of any particular crop, they would occasionally pay some farmers *not* to farm. The New Deal agriculture programs were wholly unfit for a modern market economy, and if the Republican devotion to smaller government stood for anything, it was in favor of dismantling such a system.[62]

A confluence of factors in addition to the GOP takeover of Congress made this reform possible. One of them was the particularly unique economic environment of the mid-1990s. In 1996, higher commodity prices had boosted farm incomes and, hence, decreased the political demand for subsidies. Indeed, direct government payments to farmers were lower in 1995 than they had been in over a decade.[63] While Kasich wasn't able to get some of the agricultural committee heads to help him restrain spending on farm programs in 1995, by the next year, sparking a movement to end farm welfare once and for all turned out to be feasible. Even after softening their stance against Big Government during the government shutdown, there was still some fight left in the GOP leaders to make agricultural policy reform a reality.

The premise of the Freedom to Farm Act was a phase-down of price supports over a seven-year period. At the end of that period the subsidies would basically disappear. But, as we've already seen with various other attempts to eliminate government programs over time, the programs slated for termination usually do not disappear. In just two more years, the phase-down of crop supports would be abandoned by Republicans.

Along with welfare reform, the Freedom to Farm Act and the substantial cut in nondefense discretionary spending were real accomplishments of the Republican Revolution. Ten years later, the only reform that had survived intact was that of the welfare system. That's because on the heels of the 1996 election, the GOP began to beat a hasty retreat from many of the most substantial accomplishments of their first two years in office. The party of Reagan was about to get a Big Government makeover.

THE SMELL
OF MARBLE

Gingrich and the Boys Go Native

When the Republicans assumed control of Congress in 1995, former senator Howard Baker of Tennessee, the Republican majority leader during Reagan's first term, told some members of the revolutionary freshman class a story. It dated back to the days when Baker was first elected to the US Senate in 1966.

During his first few days in the Senate, Baker was approached by Senator Norris Cotton, the senior senator from New Hampshire, whom Baker described as a "fierce-looking, pipe-smoking, hardheaded New Englander." The veteran politician asked Baker whether he could smell the marble.

Baker, a bit perplexed and intimidated, replied, "I didn't know marble had a smell."

"Well, white marble, the kind around here, does," said Cotton. "And when you can smell it, you'll like it. And you'll be ruined for life."[1]

By 1997, many members of the Republican congressional majority could smell the marble. And they liked it, too. They had "gone native," as they say. They were no longer interested in fighting Big Government. Instead, they were starting to warm to the idea of making peace with it and even enjoy keeping it around.

The transformation of the GOP into a party of Big

Government did not begin suddenly upon the inauguration of George W. Bush. Instead, it was a years-long process with its roots in the years following the 1996 midterm elections.

THE GANG OF ELEVEN

The Republican leadership was surprisingly gun-shy in a target-rich environment at the beginning of the 105th Congress. The opening days show how little interest there was in fighting Big Government among GOP leaders. Upon being reelected as Speaker, Newt Gingrich gave an acceptance speech based on promoting what he envisioned as the new "great mission" for Republicans: saving poverty-stricken children from hopelessness, violence, ignorance, racism, and drugs.[2]

Gone were the calls for a smaller government.

Gone were the acknowledgements that the federal welfare state with its barracks-like public housing projects and top-heavy education bureaucracy was the biggest impediment to economic and social advancement for inner-city youth.

In its place were muddle-headed platitudes that didn't sound very Republican. The lack of a coherent agenda led Paul Gigot of the *Wall Street Journal* to wonder if the centerpiece of the legislative agenda for the next two years was a "Contract with Ambivalence."[3] By March, the malaise had not abated. Joe Scarborough of Florida, at that point a sophomore congressman, summed up the feeling of the hard-charging True Believers of the 1994 freshman class: "Quite a few members are obviously concerned over the direction that the leadership has taken in these first three months. We have a concern that our leadership remains shell-shocked from the government shutdown a year and a half ago. Most of us are ready for them to start leading again rather than sitting back and reading from Clinton's song sheet."[4]

What afflicted the GOP leadership wasn't a lack of direction. Gingrich did have a direction in mind. The problem was that it led away from smaller government. Gingrich could smell the marble now. As *Weekly Standard* editor, William Kristol, observed, "He seems to be trying to rehabilitate himself personally instead of leading the conservative movement. He's not trying to be an ideological leader; he's trying to be a nice guy."[5]

So the fiscal conservatives in Congress sensed it was even more important to hang together now that the leadership was obviously going soft. Republicans were working with a narrower majority of eight seats this time, not twelve as in 1994. Sticking together as a consistent core of votes for smaller government might be the best hope they had. So the core group of budget cutters—John Shadegg of Arizona, Steve Largent and Tom Coburn of Oklahoma, and Mark Souder of Indiana—all took offices near each other on the fourth floor of the Cannon House Office Building. These sophomore congressmen were the core of what, along with seven other conservatives, eventually became known as the Gang of Eleven.

The Gang had their first chance to fire a legislative warning shot in late March 1997 at the bill to fund the committees of the House. The legislation would have trashed a key element of the Contract with America. In 1995, the House cut congressional committee funding by a third and celebrated one of the first Contract promises kept. Now the leadership was asking for a 14% increase in committee budgets and a $7.9 million "reserve fund" to boot. When the fund was compared to a "slush fund" by Democrats and skeptical Republicans, David Dreier of California—a close associate of Gingrich—tried to allay concern by saying it was really more like a "cookie jar" than a slush fund.[6]

The fund was supposed to be available to committees investigating President Clinton and his potentially illegal fundraising during the 1996 presidential campaign. But it indicated something deeper, too. It marked a change in the House Republican agenda, one that would motivate the party leaders for the next two years. Instead of trying to head into the 1998 midterm congressional elections presenting a clear alternative to Big Government, the GOP leadership was instead pursuing a strategy of beating up on the president and hoping to dislodge a scandal or two.

The Gang of Eleven did believe that investigating the president was a worthwhile endeavor, but to do so while simultaneously abandoning their budget principles was just too much to swallow. "It should have come as no surprise that some of us were going to say no when they want to hire more Washington bureaucrats," said budget hawk and Gang member Mark Neumann of Wisconsin. "When we go out and tell our people we're going to balance the budget, we can't start with an increase in our own budget."[7] With all Democrats opposed to the bill, the swing votes came from the eleven budget hawks. It went down to defeat by a narrow margin of three votes.

Gingrich was furious. A few minutes after the vote, he announced an unusual mandatory meeting of all House Republicans in the caucus room right outside the House chamber.

The session was going to begin with a roll call, and the Speaker threatened to send the sergeant-at-arms to round up any absent GOP congressmen.

Once the meeting started, Gingrich laid into the Gang, "The eleven geniuses who thought they knew more than the rest of the Congress are going to come up and explain their votes." It was an unusual step and one that seemed to be motivated mostly by anger. It even surprised the more senior members of Congress, none of whom had ever heard of anyone being asked to explain their vote in this way to the entire caucus. Gingrich's goal was to humiliate, and he derisively referred to the Gang as "you conservatives," like they were a distinctly different and unacceptable breed of Republican. He derided the dissenters for not being team players and threatened to delay a two-week recess until each Gang member explained himself and until the leadership had enough votes to pass the committee bill.

The first to speak was Steve Largent, former wide receiver for the Seattle Seahawks. The first words out of his mouth were, "Mr. Speaker, I am not intimidated." A hush fell over the crowd. "I have been in rooms much smaller than this one when I was on the opposite side of teammates during a player's strike against the NFL," Largent continued. "The guys in those rooms weighed 280 [or] 320 pounds and not only *wanted* to kill me, if they had gotten a hold of me they probably *could* have. That isn't the case here tonight.

"The Speaker tonight talked about the eleven of us letting the team down. The more significant question and the question that never gets asked in Washington, DC, is whose teams are we on? When I was elected to represent the first district of Oklahoma,

I wasn't elected to represent just the Republican or Democratic teams, but what I thought was in the best interest of the taxpayers back home."

Many in the room began to nod their heads, and Largent dug in some more. "Many of us were elected in 1994, and before that election we signed a document called the Contract with America. One of its pledges was to cut Washington committee funding by one third. We kept our word and did just that. Yet this proposal would reverse that cut," Largent concluded. "Whatever we do, we shouldn't do what was proposed today, which typified the Washington way of doing business so many came here to change—take credit for cutting by a third and then below the radar screen quietly add back the spending."[8]

In his recollection of this event, Tom Coburn of Oklahoma notes that Largent had clearly won over the crowd. The mood had turned against Gingrich. When he was done speaking, Largent received enthusiastic applause from most of the Republicans present.

Gingrich never tried a stunt like that again.

Instead, the Speaker worked behind the scenes to upset the plans of the fiscal conservatives. He struck a deal with the Gang to freeze committee budgets for thirty days so a compromise could eventually be reached. But instead of negotiating in good faith with the conservatives, Gingrich used the thirty-day period to cut deals with a handful of Republicans eager to increase spending. In the end, the committee budgets went up by roughly the amount originally proposed, and the cookie jar fund was also created. But the budget hawks had made their point. They would break ranks with the team whenever the coach asked them to run the ball toward the wrong end of the field. It's something that would happen again very soon.

THE BUDGET SELLOUT

When it came time to write a new federal budget for the year, it was obvious almost immediately that Gingrich and Senate majority leader Trent Lott wanted to avoid a fight with Clinton. At the time, the lead budget hawk in the Senate was Senator Phil Gramm of Texas. To try to head off any quick capitulation by Lott in the budget negotiations with Clinton, Gramm and nine other senators signed a letter that was sent to the majority leader.

"A budget deal that violates our fundamental principles is worse than no budget deal at all," the letter read. Among other demands were a commitment to steadily declining deficits and a freeze on discretionary spending. Gramm knew it was going to be a tough battle and that his main opposition wasn't going to come from the Democrats. "I'm concerned not just about the president, I'm concerned about our own negotiators," noted Gramm. "Spending money is popular."[9]

The House conservatives shared the concern. David McIntosh of Indiana explained to the *New York Times* that the grassroots were already starting to get fed up with the GOP on spending issues. There wasn't even a budget agreement yet, but there was already a feeling of betrayal in Republican circles based on the actions that had been taken in the first three slow months of 1997: rejection of a constitutional amendment on term limits, a tax hike on airline tickets, and a retreat by Gingrich on cutting the National Endowment of the Arts funding. "When people go home, our Republican base is saying, 'What are you doing?'" said McIntosh. "That's not what we sent a Republican Congress there to do."[10]

In May, while the GOP leaders and the president were banging out a budget deal, the congressional bean-counters discovered a revenue windfall of up to $225 billion over five years—$45 billion for 1997 alone—as a result of the unexpectedly strong economy. Suddenly a new fight broke out between the GOP leaders and Clinton, only this time it was over where to spend the new cash. Virtually every constituency got what they wanted except the budget cutters. It was more than enough to spur Senator Phil Gramm to note that "the era of big government is alive and well and guaranteed in Washington, DC, . . . This is the kind of budget that comes about when the two great political parties stop debating ideas and start conspiring against the public."[11]

"It is a budget of concession and illusion," said Republican senator Rod Grams of Minnesota. "Like a house of cards, it is made out of nothing and held together by nothing but wishes and assumptions."[12] A look at the numbers shows Grams was being charitable. The GOP leadership was claiming the budget deal amounted to a spending cut. But those cuts wouldn't occur until after 2000, and it would likely only occur on paper. If there's anything that the fiscal conservatives had learned it's that the promises of future budget cuts are just as bad as no cuts at all. When it comes time to eat the spinach, Congress always finds an excuse to leave the table.

The 1997 budget deal itself was replete with political retreats. In the Contract with America budget, all categories of spending that Republicans said they wanted to slice were slated for budget cuts every year through 2002. Now, two years later, those trends were reversed. The old spending caps were abandoned, and budget trends were now moving in the other direction. The 1997 deal ended up hiking discretionary spending by $29 billion over the Contract with America budget cap through 1998, an 11.5% increase over what Republicans would have spent if they hadn't retreated.

The GOP talking points on the budget compromise reminded reporters that the agreement gave Clinton less than he'd asked for. That's certainly true. But Republicans voluntarily gave up more of their own territory than Clinton did. In February, the president had asked for $287 billion in nondefense discretionary spending for that year. The Republican leadership agreed to a budget that actually spent $282 billion for those programs. Meanwhile, if they had simply stuck to the Contract with America budget, spending on those programs would have been only $253 billion. Yes, rubber-stamping Clinton's budget would have resulted in $5 billion more in nondefense discretionary spending. But the GOP happily agreed to spend $29 billion more that year than they said they would in 1995.

The main selling point for many Republicans was the tax cuts in the agreement. The tax cuts were the first since Reagan's historic income tax cut of 1981. Among the new cuts was a supply-siders dream: a reduction in the capital gains tax rate from 28% to 20%. It would make the tax code more investment-friendly by lowering the cost of capital. It was very Reaganesque and represented just the sort of thing that Republicans always said should be the guidepost of any good tax plan.

But there were other tax cuts in the agreement, too. There was a $500 per-child tax credit—strongly supported by the Christian and profamily groups—and a Clinton proposal to provide tax credits for college tuition. These credits were a departure from standard Republican tax policy doctrine—especially among supporters of a clean, flat income tax—which viewed tax credits as a needless complication of the tax code. It struck some of the fiscal conservatives as just another attempt to buy off certain political constituencies.

Yet the tax cuts were the only reason many fiscal conservatives, who initially expressed their dismay over the spending increases, eventually voted for the budget agreement. Still, it was evident many of them were holding their noses while doing it. "[The GOP will] do anything to get some tax cuts," complained Representative Tom Coburn. He realized the tax cuts were a "pittance" and the spending cuts would not materialize.[13]

Even John Kasich was backed into an awkward position by the deal. As the GOP point-man on the budget, it was his job to defend the deal publicly, but his allies among the fiscal conservatives sensed he wasn't entirely happy with it. When Coburn ran into Kasich in Statuary Hall in the Capitol one afternoon that summer, the doctor from Oklahoma could tell "by the look of resignation on [Kasich's] face that he wasn't going to get what he wanted [in the budget deal]."

"Tom," said Kasich in a slightly defensive tone, "it's the best we could get."[14]

The discontent of grassroots Republicans was beginning to bubble up. The Texas GOP chairman told the *Washington Times* that the congressional majority "was fudging the differences

between Republicans and Democrats . . . Conservatives are getting very frustrated at the grass-roots level. This looks like a
[budget] deal that doesn't change much, and people want something bold."[15] Veteran political journalist Robert Novak reported
that many of the deep-pocket sources of Republican funding
were also unhappy. The usually reliable ticket-buyers for the
$1,000-a-plate fundraising gala at the Washington Hilton were
declining the invitations. And on the first business day after the
budget deal was announced, the switchboard of the Republican
national headquarters was swamped with calls from rank-and-rile
GOP voters protesting the budget "sellout." Some even threatened to cease their contributions to the party immediately or
demanded to be removed from the mailing lists.[16]

Some Republican congressmen who voted for the plan found
themselves getting an earful of grief from their constituents. As
one of the charter members of the Gang of Eleven, John Shadegg,
put it, "There's no sizzle in bragging about what we did."[17] Some
Republicans even found they had political challenges on their
hands as a result of their support for the budget deal. When
Representative Bob Inglis of South Carolina started his campaign
to unseat Fritz Hollings, the long-time incumbent Democratic
senator, he had an unexpected challenger in the GOP primary to
overcome first. A party activist from Greenville named Stephen
Brown made Inglis' support for the final budget deal the centerpiece of his protest candidacy. "That was the straw that broke the
camel's back," said Brown. "The whole balanced-budget deal is a
sham."[18] Surprisingly, Brown ended up winning three of four
regional straw polls in October 1997. Inglis won the GOP nomination—and eventually lost the Senate race—but Brown's

candidacy was a reminder of the discontent among conservative voters within the Republican Party.

When a budget surplus materialized in fiscal 1998—four years before anyone expected it—senior Republicans were quick to suggest that the 1997 budget deal was the vehicle that brought the country to the promised land of a balanced budget. What really brought the budget into balance, however, was an unexpectedly strong economy.

In fact, the 1997 budget deal was actually a step back in terms of fiscal discipline. The budget was balanced in spite of the 1997 budget agreement, not because of it. If the Republicans had simply stuck with the discretionary spending levels outlined in the Contract with America budget of 1995, they would have not only been able to balance the budget in 1998, but the federal government would have found itself with a surplus of $104 billion. Instead, the 1997 budget deal put spending on a new upward trajectory that, while still achieving overall balance by 1998, whittled the first-year surplus down to $69 billion.

It's also worth noting that the surplus was mainly a product of an accounting gimmick in place since 1969. The only reason the federal government had a surplus at all in 1998 was that it collected $99 billion more in payroll tax revenue than was needed to pay Social Security benefits. This allowed Congress and the White House to paper over the $30 billion *deficit* in the non-Social Security part of the budget. A comparison to what might have been if Congress had simply stuck to the Contract with America budget is again apt. An *actual* on-budget surplus of $4.8 billion would have materialized if the old spending caps were kept intact. Again, the claims of success by supporters of the 1997 budget proved to be overblown.

But if there's one thing that can be counted on in Washington, it's partisanship. The Republican leadership, despite caving in to Clinton in so many areas, was still able to muster enough political will to stop just short of giving Clinton everything he wanted. As long as a Democrat was the one advocating increases in many government programs, his proposals had a marginally higher hurdle to clear than the programs being pushed by Republicans. Clinton pushed back equally hard on the GOP's favored programs in response. Thus, a soft form of gridlock ensued.

This tended to dampen government growth. When compared to where it could have been if Republicans had stuck to the Contract with America budget, things looked grim. But when compared to where spending could have gone if Democrats controlled Congress, the GOP came out looking better. Republicans were able to resist a total of $28 billion of Clinton's proposed increases in nondefense discretionary programs between 1995 and 1997. That number grew to $47 billion by the end of Clinton's presidency. This form of soft gridlock slowed the rate of government growth and put an outer boundary on how much territory Republicans were willing to give up. That's at least a small consolation—perhaps the only one—in the wake of such quick retreats by the GOP after 1996.

Ironically, the success in temporarily slowing the rate of budget growth presented a new ally to Big Government. What happened next is what you would probably expect if you've already noticed the pattern of the tale being told here. Instead of using the revenue windfall as an opportunity to start fundamentally reforming entitlements programs like Social Security—something that everyone agreed needed to be done—or cut taxes, the budget surplus set off a political shopping spree.

The first stage came in the form of a gargantuan highway bill.

THE ROAD TO HELL

As the ink was drying on the 1997 budget deal, Pennsylvania congressman Bud Shuster, the powerful Infrastructure and Transportation Committee chairman, was itching to get his $102 billion, six-year highway bill onto the floor of the House. But Gingrich persuaded him to wait.

Still smarting from the criticism of fiscal conservatives over the newly-passed budget, Gingrich knew it would look bad to give his blessing to a bill that would blow right through the already generous spending caps set in the budget deal. So Shuster agreed to sit on the bill until the spring of 1998.

That Gingrich's concerns were more tactical than principled is evident in his own memoirs. Gingrich wrote that he thought the bill was "meritorious" but also that the GOP "was in real danger of looking like a bunch of fools or hypocrites if we turned around and brought out a massive, multibillion dollar, multi-year bill that destroyed the spending ceilings we had just written into law."[19]

The delay proved to be a blessing to Shuster. By the time spring of 1998 rolled around, the growing economy had filled out the fuel tax coffers, and the pot of money he had to play with had more than doubled to $218 billion. It was enough to further raise the hackles of the House fiscal conservatives who were still sore from the 1997 budget debacle. This time, how-ever, they had their old ally John Kasich back on their side of the battle lines.

Kasich came out firing against the highway bill, which he called a "hog" and an "abomination."[20] "I'm worried we are not about changing the culture [of spending] in Washington," the budget chairman said. "I get concerned that we are like a boxer in the fifth round who has tasted his blood a little and doesn't want to get up off the stool."[21] When Kasich pleaded with other House leaders to cut the rate of growth of the highway bill in half, he was overruled by Gingrich.[22] Instead, the Speaker was content to let the bill bust through the budget spending caps by $26 billion.[23]

Now that the price had been determined, all that was left was to make the shopping list. Shuster needed to find a way to neutralize the opposition. There were some means of persuasion Shuster could employ. One of them was the oldest trick in the book. He would try to buy their support.

On 17 March 1998, one of Shuster's aids left a voicemail for Tom Coburn's transportation staffer: "We have a deal on the funding levels for [the highway bill]. I originally spoke to your boss, to your office, last September and we had notified you that there was $10 million in the bill for your boss. We're upping that by $5 million, so you have $15 million, and I'm just trying to figure out where you want to put the new money, the new $5 million."[24] Coburn refused the offer and made a copy of the voicemail.

Over the next few days, other congressmen received similar calls. Lindsey Graham of South Carolina was offered $15 million for projects on 19 March, and he had until 5:00 PM to decide if he wanted to accept the offer. He declined and then alerted the media about this unseemly attempt to persuade him to support the bill. "Of all the things I've been unhappy with that were done by the leadership, this was the worst. It violates all our principles."[25] Steve Largent told a press conference that he was offered the same sort of deal. "I told them my vote is not for sale," he boomed.[26] Sue Myrick of New York told ABC News that she was offered $15 million in projects, too. ABC also played a tape of the voicemail that Coburn's office received.

Shuster went ballistic. He immediately sent the word out that if any congressmen talked to a reporter about what had been offered, their piece of the action would be taken back. Then he turned around and vehemently told reporters, "I have not spoken to anybody about getting their votes."[27]

Over the next few weeks, more details of the offers made to various congressmen to support the bill began to trickle out. It turns out that the approach Shuster and the leadership took to gather support for the bill was quite systematic. There was a pecking order to how generous the offer of spoils would be. House members facing a tough reelection bid could get $20 million to $30 million. Transportation Committee members, who were already supporting the bill, helped themselves to an average of $40 million. Everyone else was offered $15 million, and even that was negotiable if you put up a fuss.[28]

On 26 March 1998, Shuster took to the House floor and gave a bizarre speech that compared the charges that he tried to buy votes to Joseph McCarthy's claim that there were fifty-seven communist agents working in the federal government in 1950.

"Well, he got lots of headlines, but, of course, he was eventually proved to be a liar. I am reminded of that event, although I certainly make no such charge here today."

He then went on to claim that his House critics had actually submitted projects to him to be included in the bill. But the chairman was unfairly comparing two different sorts of requests and he knew it. Coburn and the others had simply sent along to Shuster a list of programs that were requested by their states' departments of transportation. It was standard procedure for a bill like this. After all, the fuel tax had been collected from the states, so it was common practice to confer with them about where the money should be spent within each state.

What Shuster and his staff were offering to members of Congress in exchange for their support of the bill was qualitatively different: absolute control over a chunk of money and a set of projects that didn't require consultation with or approval of state-level policymakers. Want to build an expensive, unrequested bridge and name it after yourself? Go ahead. Want to build a road that helps you get to that new estate you just purchased? Here's your chance. What Shuster was offering were funds for outright boondoggles. And the budget hawks were not interested in that.

The next day, John Kasich joined a group of the insurgents at a press conference and openly defied Newt Gingrich by announcing his intent to help kill the bill. "We came to Washington to change the culture of this town and frankly this bill . . . is a significant detour from where our party has been going." On Fox News a few days before the vote, he declared, "This bill is [a] throwback to the old ways. This is one where we fell down . . . I just hope we don't get comfortable with governing in this way, because if we do, we wouldn't be any better than the way Democrats ran the place."[29]

The day of the vote was punctuated by a series of tense and emotional speeches from the fiscal conservatives. They rose to denounce the process as "corrupt" and a betrayal of the Republican Revolution. When Kasich and Lindsey Graham introduced an amendment to defund the pork projects, they were defeated by a four-to-one margin. In the end, only eighty congressmen voted against the highway bill.

The budget hawks were ultimately successful at getting the GOP leadership some bad press, and the amount spent on pork projects in the final version of the bill totaled $9.3 billion, down from $11 billion. But that is still over 50% more than the amount spent on pork projects in the previous highway bill in 1991. The number of overall projects had grown by mind-boggling amounts, too. Whereas the 1991 bill only had 538 of these sorts of projects, the 1998 bill had 1,850. That was twelve times the number of pork projects that were in the highway bill that Reagan vetoed in 1987.[30]

These projects ranged from the ridiculous to the absurd. To name just a few:

- $7 million for a transportation museum in Allentown, Pennsylvania.

- $3 million for a documentary on "infrastructure awareness."

- $500,000 to study sidewalks at the Kennedy Center.

- $1.5 million to research the packing habits of truckers.[31]

When Reagan vetoed the 1987 highway bill, he said he hadn't seen so much lard since he handed out blue ribbons at the Iowa State Fair. Yet here Republicans were, just over ten years later, presiding over an even more monstrous piece of legislation. And they weren't done yet. There were still a few months left before the 1998 congressional elections. There was still more surplus money to spend.

THE SPENDING SPREE OF 1998

John Kasich felt the GOP had to reassume the small-government stance of the Republican Revolution and had to do it quickly or, as Kasich saw it, risk potential disaster in the 1998 midterm elections. So, he pulled together a budget plan the likes of which hadn't been seen since 1995.

One that eliminated the Departments of Commerce and Energy.

One that picked up and dusted off many of the budget cuts that were ditched after the leaders turned their backs on the Contract with America budget.

One that cut taxes by $100 billion over five years and included $154 billion in spending cuts to offset the tax cuts and at least a portion of the bloated highway bill.[32]

The goal was to get the money out of Washington before politicians had a chance to spend it, while also getting rid of a bunch of federal programs in the process. In short, a true reduction in the size and scope of government.

Then just over a week after Kasich unveiled his plan in late April, the Congressional Budget Office reported that the surplus

for 1998 was going to be about $40 billion bigger than origi-
nally estimated.[33] The news provided just the excuse the GOP
leadership needed to avoid launching another attack on Big
Government. They had already achieved victory over the deficit,
so why not redirect all the new money to programs they liked
while they had the chance?

When Kasich presented his budget plan to the leadership,
even he was surprised at the trashing it got. In a closed-door meeting, Gingrich took to task the back-bencher conservatives who
were continually demanding budget cuts. Robert Livingston,
chairman of the Appropriations Committee and perennial opponent of spending cuts, raged at Kasich's audacity. He even suggested that as an appropriator it was his job to spend money and
he simply had no choice but to do so. The budget chairman
wasn't even able to get Tom DeLay, number three in the House
GOP command and often a vocal supporter of Kasich, to come to
his defense this time. Instead, DeLay sat mute, as the Republican
leaders beat up Kasich's plan.

Kasich left the meeting even more disheartened than before it
started. The leadership was clearly opting for a strategy of attack-
ing the president on his questionable ethics while simultaneously
stealing a page from Clinton's playbook—expanding government
through incremental increases to pet programs and showering
key special interests with the newfound taxpayer money.

After the meeting, Kasich turned to a colleague and uttered
the words he never thought would cross his lips: "They don't want
to cut government."[34]

What came next was enough to convince even the most wild-
eyed GOP partisan that Kasich was right. A few weeks before the

midterm elections of 1998, the Republican Congress approved a budget that hiked nondefense discretionary spending by over 5% for that year—over twice as much as the 1997 budget deal—and funded a record amount of pork-barrel projects. It was in every way a rout of the very ideals that won the GOP a majority in Congress in the first place.

It contained $18 billion in additional bailout money for the foreign aid operations of the International Monetary Fund just weeks after the IMF conceded that the $5 billion it had already given to Russia had been stolen by corrupt political leaders.[35] There was $1.1 billion for home heating subsidies; $10 million for moving a Cape Hatteras lighthouse 2,000 feet inland; $5 million in military construction money for a car wash, a movie theater, and a day-care center in Fairbanks, Alaska; $1 million for peanut research in Dawson, Georgia, and Raleigh, North Carolina; $2 million for "culinary and cultural arts" projects in Missouri; $1 million for "peanut quality research;" and $5 million for "wood utilization research." Even Senator Robert Byrd of West Virginia, known in the halls of the Senate as the "Prince of Pork," called the bill a "gargantuan monstrosity."[36]

The budget also funded $20 billion in so-called "emergency" expenditures. Usually these sorts of appropriations are passed to fund unanticipated spending like disaster relief. But the 1998 bill was different. Most of the emergency spending was clearly unnecessary or at least certainly not worthy of being called an emergency. Much of it consisted of more pork-barrel projects, particularly water and energy projects in key congressional districts. Even the expense of conducting the 2000 census was deemed an emergency, despite the fact that it's hardly unexpected on account of it being constitutionally mandated every ten years.[37] The $20 billion spent on these so-called emergencies was the most money appropriated in this way since 1991. In that year, the emergency spending went to fund the Gulf War.[38]

Why was this spending deemed an emergency? Because emergency expenditures don't count against the budget caps. So Congress and the president were able to bust the budget by $20 billion simply by assigning those particular expenses a specific name and then pretending the spending never occurred. It wouldn't even show up on the federal books until after it was spent. That freed up $20 billion more to play with.

The 1998 budget also hiked farm subsidies and violated the Freedom to Farm Act of 1996, one of the grandest achievements of the Republican Revolution. That year alone, the budget doubled price supports for farmers.[39] As Republican senator Richard Lugar of Indiana, a long-time opponent of federal farm programs, said, "It didn't matter what it was. Any appropriator sitting around the table threw it in for good measure."[40] The budget added new handouts for dairy farmers and wool producers and resurrected a program to subsidize mohair producers. The last was the most odious to small-government conservatives. The original mohair subsidy, terminated in 1995, was originally created to hold down the cost of military uniforms during World War II. But the Army and Navy haven't used mohair uniforms since the Korean War. Yet, taxpayers were now being forced to spend millions of dollars to pad the profit margins of mohair makers in 1998 and 1999.

Clinton got much of what he wanted, too. Republicans enthusiastically embraced the president's proposal to spend $1.1

billion to hire 100,000 new teachers as a way to reduce class sizes, despite the fact that Republicans used to believe it wasn't their job to expand the role of the federal government in education—and the even savvier ones knew that extensive studies showed class sizes had no bearing on educational achievement.[41]

The conventional wisdom is that the Republicans changed their tune, because they were afraid of alienating voters who construed being opposed to education funding as akin to being opposed to educational progress. While it's true GOP leaders were cagey about the party's image on education, its newfound love of education funding was really part of an overall shift toward a love for all sorts of federal programs. And it was all made possible by the federal budget surplus. As we'll see later, this spend-whatever-you-can-and-then-some-more approach to education policy in particular would reach its apex during the presidency of George W. Bush. But it has its roots in 1997 and 1998 as a byproduct of the overall GOP abandonment of limited government principles.

Defenders of Gingrich like to point out that these shifts, while they look like political retreats on the surface, were really necessary trade-offs for increased spending on more important Republican priorities, in particular national security and intelligence. As Fox News' Major Garrett has reported, Gingrich agreed to give Clinton an extra $20 billion in domestic spending over five years in exchange for $20 billion in increases in top-secret intelligence budgets. As John Feehery, spokesman for current Speaker Dennis Hastert, told Garrett, "There's no way we would have gotten that intelligence money without [the 1998 budget bill]. And nobody knew about it. And most people don't know about it now. They just assumed we caved for no reason."[42]

Yet this defense rings hollow when you consider the Republicans were caving in a full year before that.

Besides, Gingrich was hardly leading by example. He did not eschew his own pork projects to make way for more spending on high-priority national security needs. He successfully earmarked $450 million in the budget for seven C-130J transport planes, even though the Pentagon said it wanted only one.[43] The planes were made by Lockheed-Martin in Marietta, Georgia, which just happened to be in his district.

Gingrich could have helped Kasich and the conservatives push for offsetting the increase in intelligence spending by cutting pork-barrel spending or lower-priority programs. But the Speaker fought the small government supporters on that, too. Tom Coburn notes in his memoirs that Gingrich and Livingston essentially nixed the idea of offsetting cuts when the idea was presented to them by Coburn and eleven other fiscal conservatives in the House.[44]

In fact, some of the spending on national security and the war on drugs was unnecessary. Senator Ted Stevens of Alaska slipped into the bill $1 billion for ballistic missile defense. When asked by the media about it, the Pentagon brass said they were "bewildered" by Stevens' actions. The army's theater missile defense program had been plagued with failures, and the Department of Defense said they really couldn't use the money anyway. The FBI got a $40 million Gulfstream jet they'd never asked for in the first place. And the Agricultural Research Service spent most of that November trying to figure out what it was going to do with an unexpected and unrequested six-fold increase in its drug-war budget.[45]

The final bill cost $500 billion, had almost 4,000 pages, weighed forty pounds, and was prepared so hastily and released so close to the floor vote that it was read by virtually no member of Congress. Gingrich took to the floor before the vote to denounce the "perfectionist caucus" who thought the bill was too bloated.[46] It was obvious whom he was talking about.

The bill passed 333 to 95 in the House and 65 to 29 in the GOP Senate. The ironic part is that the bill won mainly because more Democrats than Republicans voted for it.[47] It was all enough to leave a bad taste in the mouth of the already down-trodden House conservatives. "I remember reading about all these Christmas-tree bills before I came to Congress and being disgusted," said Mark Sanford of South Carolina. "And now we're ending up here." Even Representative Jim Moran, a Virginia Democrat and certainly no fiscal conservative, moaned about it: "I knew the closer you got to election day, the more stuff was going to get dumped into [the omnibus bill]. There was enough money for farmers to buy both of the Dakotas. Everybody got just about everything they wanted."[48]

The bill included 2,839 pork projects, a new record—much higher than the 958 earmarks in the GOP's 1995 budget. It amounted to almost twice the number of projects (1,439) in the final budget passed by the last Democratic Congress in 1994.

Conservatives were already pondering whether a world without a Republican congressional majority would be all that bad. As George Will speculated in an October 1998 column, "It is unclear that having more Republicans in Congress would be good for either the Constitution or conservatism."[49]

Two weeks before Election Day, Gingrich predicted that Republicans would gain anywhere between ten and forty seats. Even Democrats were pessimistic about their chances in the midterm elections. Although they quibbled with Gingrich's estimate, Democratic Party officials still expected their party would lose at least a small handful of seats.[50]

Everyone was wrong. Republicans lost three seats, narrowing their majority to five votes in the House. Exit polls showed that turnout for self-identified conservatives dropped 6% from 1994 to 1998 and that support of GOP among self-identified independent voters dropped by 7%.[51] This may not sound like a lot, but consider this: Republican House candidates received a total of 32 million votes, and all Democratic candidates received 31 million votes. That's a difference of about 2%.[52] In a race that close, Republicans needed the help of self-identified fiscal conservative voters. But those voters were clearly peeved that Republicans had lost their fiscal backbone and decided to stay home on Election Day.

Gingrich resigned as Speaker three days later.

MEET THE NEW BOSS, SAME AS THE OLD BOSS

For the Republicans, 1999 should have been a time for a fresh start. They installed Dennis Hastert of Illinois as the new Speaker of the House. He was liked by many on both sides of the aisle and was seen mostly as a technician, devoted to making sure the legislative trains ran on time.

But it didn't seem as if there was much fight in the new boss to control federal spending. When asked about whether Congress would stick to the budget caps that year, Hastert provided a wishy-washy response: "I am not saying we are going to bust them, or that we are not going to bust them." Yet the caps were the last line in the stand for conservatives. "Once you let the caps go, the fiscal discipline goes out the window," said David McIntosh of Indiana, one of the original Gang of Eleven.[53]

The budget surplus was still expanding rapidly. John Kasich knew the pressure would be on to bust the caps, so he made it his goal to keep them intact. "We are not going to blow [the surplus] by spending it on Big Government," he said.[54] Even President Clinton wanted to look like he was sticking to the caps, but his spending request had to use a series of accounting gimmicks to do it. Republicans were quick to call it a smoke-and-mirrors budget.[55]

When the Senate and the House agreed on a spending blueprint that kept the budget limits intact, the GOP trumpeted the agreement as a claim to the moral high-ground.[56] Yet all they were doing was agreeing to keep the promise they made to fiscal conservatives two years previously. Only in Washington is failure to break a promise considered a saintly act of integrity.

Despite what the press reported at the time, maintaining the caps would not require spending cuts. Spending would still go up by about 1%. But because of the pretzel logic of baseline budgeting—wherein a smaller-than-expected increase is considered a budget decrease—the supporters of Big Government were starting to chafe under the supposedly strict caps. With each new estimate of the ballooning surplus from the Congressional Budget Office, the big spenders could hardly contain their glee. The first couple of bills Congress passed that year included a military pay increase of three times the rate of inflation and an emergency spending package for the war in Kosovo that was loaded with pork projects.[57]

Tom Coburn of Oklahoma decided it was time to wage guerilla warfare. He warned the appropriators that he would hold the budget process hostage by offering 115 amendments to cut spending in various programs within the agricultural bill. By House rules, each amendment was entitled to five minutes of debate. That amounts to ten hours, or two legislative days. Coburn predicted he wouldn't win any of the amendments— and he was right—but he was trying to make a point. Gumming up the works finally got the attention of Speaker Hastert, who promised the fiscal conservatives that he would make sure the budget bills stuck to the spending caps. Coburn called off his de facto filibuster.[58]

And that's when business-as-usual resumed. By the end of the summer—less than seven months after denouncing Clinton's budget as replete with accounting gimmicks—the Republican leadership was already evading the caps by using the old trick of designating $22 billion in spending as an emergency, including more funds for the 2000 census, and fuel assistance for the poor.[59] They also found a nifty way of giving the US its first thirteen-month year by allowing federal agencies to spend money in the current year but not enter it on the books until immediately after the last day of the twelfth month of the fiscal year.[60] When asked by reporters from the *Washington Post* about this peculiar move, Senate Appropriations Chairman Ted Stevens of Alaska stated flatly, "There's no smoke and mirrors in our budget at all."[61]

Kasich launched a last-ditch campaign to get a 2.7% across-the-board cut to bring spending back under the budget caps.[62] But by the end of the year, the cut had been whittled down to 0.38%, and it applied to such a small portion of the budget that Republican leaders conceded it was mostly symbolic.[63]

Meanwhile, Congress passed and Clinton signed into law another farm bailout package. This one cost $8.7 billion, up from the $6 billion package the previous year. It hoisted subsidies to almost three times what they were supposed to cost under the Freedom to Farm Act. That was par for the course for the rest of the budget, too. When all was said and done, discretionary spending ended up $51 billion above the spending cap and it wasn't even an election year.[64]

The political spin that followed the passage of the budget indicated that a majority of the Republicans and its leadership were intoxicated by the smell of the marble in the Capitol. The National Republican Congressional Committee sent out a press release that attacked seven Democrats—not for being big spenders but for actually opposing spending projects in the Interior Department appropriations bill. The press release quoted Tom DeLay, the House Majority whip, as saying, "In all my years in Congress this is a first: a member of Congress actually voting against a project that would have benefited his own district." He must not have been paying attention to the actions of many of the fiscal conservatives within his own party who had been doing that for years.

The 2000 budget battle the next year was a reprise of the 1999 battle. Or, for that matter, the 1997 battle and 1998 battle. They all started with pronouncements by Republicans that their budget would stay within the caps and that Clinton's budget spent too much. Then the surplus would get bigger and so would the congressional appetite for spending. As Senator Phil Gramm astutely observed, Republicans had finally discovered an answer to the political dilemma posed by the budget surplus. "If this budget is adopted," said Gramm, "we will have found a sure-fire way to stop the Democrats from spending the surplus—have the Republicans spend it first."[65]

The year 2000 ended with another bloated budget bill. It grew by just under 6% in a year, when inflation only grew around 3%. By the end of the 106th Congress of 1999–2000, the GOP had become the biggest spending congressional majority since the Democratic Congress of 1977–1978 under Tip O'Neill, even after adjusting for inflation.

The late-1990s also exposed the weakness of focusing on deficit reduction as a political goal. Once the budget is balanced, what do you do? Without a firm commitment to reducing government spending and shrinking the role of the federal leviathan, Republicans didn't have a principled leg to stand on in their subsequent battles with Clinton. And the only reason Republicans had accomplished anything that appealed to fiscal conservatives was because of an aggressive start in 1995, a limit on further losses thanks to the inertia of divided government, and the presence of a small band of committed small-government conservatives hoping to keep the dream of limited government alive.

After 1996 and welfare reform, the leadership never again put forward a plan to lock in the gains they made in terms of budget cuts, and never advanced an agenda that took seriously the goal of scaling back Big Government. It seems inevitable in hindsight that the onset of the budget surplus would fracture the coalition of fiscal conservatives who really wanted to scale back government and a large majority of Republicans who were happy simply declaring victory over the deficit.

For John Kasich, the year 2000 marked his last stand. He had decided not to run for reelection. It was also the final year for congressmen like Tom Coburn and Mark Sanford, who had limited themselves to only three terms. It was the end of an era. There would not be another substantial conservative uprising among members of Congress until the summer of 2005. In the meantime, the Republican Party would continue its steady metamorphosis into a party of Big Government. And that transformation was about to be kicked into overdrive with the presidency of George W. Bush.

SELLING OUT

*The GOP Becomes the Party
of Big Government*

T he only hope to stop the spending is to elect George W. Bush."

No, that's not a joke. Those were the words of Representative John Shadegg of Arizona just weeks before the 2000 presidential election.[1] They neatly sum up the thinking of fiscal conservatives in the GOP that year. Republicans sensed they had reached the limits of what they could do without the White House under their control. Fiscal conservatives outside the party thought so, too. Robert Novak even devoted a chapter of a book he authored that year to why winning back the White House was an essential part of completing what the Republican Revolution of 1994 started. By the time George W. Bush won the presidency, there was a lot riding on the promise of a united Republican government.

The first self-proclaimed conservative president since Reagan, Bush would have to choose to uphold the goal of reducing the role of government or give up the fight. He chose the latter. Not even the most hardened cynic could have predicted the fiscal damage that decision would inflict.

THE BLADE AND THE VETO PEN

When President Bush chose Mitch Daniels, a senior vice president at Eli Lilly, as White House budget chief, Washington pundits were quick to point out that Daniels didn't have much experience in the sort of job he'd just been tapped for. He certainly wasn't a budget wonk with years of experience fighting for limited government on the Hill like David Stockman. His main qualification seemed to be that the president liked him and that he hailed from the private sector.

His task was ostensibly to get a handle on federal spending. Daniels certainly seemed up to the task if personal behavior was any indication. Press reports from early 2001 liked to play up his frugality. They sometimes referred to him as the "Penny Pincher in Chief," mentioned that he buys his suits off the rack, and even recounted the story of some years earlier when he fished coins from a bar toilet to pay for a pitcher of beer.[2]

Daniels tended to approach his job with humor. When members of Congress, agency heads, or lobbyists would complain to him about a White House proposal, he would have his staff send the source of the complaint a mug or a t-shirt with the phrase "Get Over It" emblazoned on it. And he tried—unsuccessfully—to get the phone system at the Office of Management and Budget to play the Rolling Stones' "You Can't Always Get What You Want" for callers on hold.[3]

There seemed to be, during the first half of 2001, a shared interest by the president in cutting spending. In the early days of the administration, insiders were telling reporters to expect the "Full Gipper," which was code for a Reaganesque policy agenda that would appeal to his conservative base of support, including cuts in spending and taxes.[4] As late as the summer of 2001, Bush was telling his Cabinet that they should cooperate with Daniels to present a united front on spending control. Since he was the guy in charge of slicing the budget, the president nicknamed him "The Blade," prompting Daniels to hang a samurai sword on his office wall.[5]

The buzz around town was that Bush's first budget would significantly slow the rate of spending.[6] The goal was to make room for the president's signature initiative: the ten-year, $1.6-trillion tax cut that Bush had campaigned on, which would at least partially reverse the Clinton tax hikes of 1993. With the Congressional Budget Office projecting a budget surplus of $5.6 trillion over the following decade—only $2.5 trillion of which would be an "off-budget" Social Security surplus—the White House would be able to give back at least half of the on-budget surplus of $3 trillion to taxpayers.[7]

The tax cuts were often justified on the grounds they would spur economic growth. At the unveiling of the plan in February 2001, Bush said it was a response to the "warning light" flashing on the "dashboard of [the] economy."[8] Economic conservatives agreed with that approach, but there was another sort of urgency for them, too. Getting the money out of Washington before it was spent was reason enough to support the tax cuts. That was partly the reason the tax plan was sent to Capitol Hill before the budget. The White House strategists believed that if the White House could rope off the surplus for tax relief, restraining spending would be that much easier. Congress would simply have less money to spend.

Daniels had his work cut out for him. As conservatives had discovered in the late 1990s, the budget surplus had turned the GOP into a party without any motivation to cut government. With a balanced budget, the main argument Republicans used to support their spending-cut agenda had disappeared. Leadership from the president on the budget would be vital.

Listening to the rhetoric coming out of the White House press office, it seemed that leadership would be forthcoming. Bush's press secretary, Ari Fleischer, rebutted criticism of the tax cut as a threat to a balanced budget by telling reporters that "the greatest danger to increasing the public debt is government spending, not tax cuts."[9]

The strategy of the Blade and the Veto Pen emerged. Daniels—the Blade—would compose the budgets, defend them before Congress and the media, and threaten a veto when necessary. The president would, if needed, publicly provide back up for Daniels by repeating the veto threat. For the White House strategy to work, however, it would have to be followed by actual vetoes.

When finally unveiled, the proposed budget pushed at least some of the right buttons for fiscal conservatives. It made small cuts in some of the programs that were targeted in the Contract with America, and it took a $12 billion swipe at corporate welfare programs, including cuts in crop subsidies by a third.[10] The budgets of the Departments of Commerce, and Housing, and Urban Development were also cut slightly from the previous year's levels.

But the overall package was not a Stockmanesque assault on the federal behemoth. There were virtually no program terminations of any consequence, just some pruning around the edges. Coming up with real cuts shouldn't be hard in a federal budget that cost about $2 trillion at the time. Daniels, however, was constrained by the president's interest in expanding large swaths of the welfare state. Candidate Bush spent much of the 2000 campaign outlining all the new programs he planned to create. Once in office, President Bush was perfectly happy keeping most current programs intact, too. The main fight he intended to launch was to freeze or slightly shrink the size of old federal programs to make way for some new ones.

Daniels was also directed to make room in the budget for two of the president's biggest proposals: a new prescription drug benefit for Medicare and a huge increase in education spending. The massive proposed increase in spending on education programs—11% after adjusting for inflation—was the largest hike in federal funding for education in twenty-six years.[11] Increases like this, along with extra money for other pet Bush projects— like subsidies to oil companies—overwhelmed the small savings that came from freezing or modestly cutting a small handful of other programs.

Total spending levels on nondefense discretionary spending would go up, not down, as they did in most of the Reagan and Kasich budget proposals.[12] The budget also proposed to bust the discretionary budget caps set out in the 1997 budget deal by at least $97 billion, something even the White House had to admit in the fine print.[13]

Meanwhile, Republicans in Congress were sounding like spendaholics who were begging for an intervention by Bush and his veto pen. Senator Judd Gregg of New Hampshire told a *Washington Post* reporter, "Congress [has] a fiscal discipline problem." He noted that the recent huge increases in spending were "supported by all segments of Republicans. . . . We have seen the enemy and he is us."[14]

Senate Finance Committee Chairman, Charles Grassley of Iowa, concluded that Bush's ability to hold the line on the budget "is directly related to the president's decisiveness on vetoing bills."[15] He certainly knew how eager members of the Senate were to spend money. The day after that quote appeared in the *Washington Post*, Grassley sponsored an amendment to the budget to add $63.5 billion in extra assistance to farmers over the next ten years. The amendment passed.[16]

The president's tax cut passed in May in a slightly reduced form. Then Senator Jim Jeffords of Vermont, apparently fed up with the Bush administration for not spending enough on education (despite the massive increase the president had proposed) and for pushing a large tax cut through Congress (which he voted for), left the GOP and handed control of the evenly-divided Senate to the Democrats. So, with the budget still far from passage, Mitch Daniels had to play hardball and step up the threat of a presidential veto if Congress didn't put the budget on a leash. "[T]he president has to sign these bills before the money goes out the door," he said.[17]

Suddenly, the economic picture began to look less rosy. The White House reported in late August that the projected budget surplus for fiscal 2002 would decline by $58 billion.[18] Most of that drop was a result of a weakening economy and higher-than-expected spending. It was going to require serious restraint to keep from tapping the Social Security surplus, something both parties claimed they didn't want to touch. But the decline was enough to spur Bush to wag a finger in the general direction of Congress and say he was "watching carefully" to guard against a "last-minute budget raid" that might spark a veto.[19] He reiterated the threat during a press conference on his Texas ranch a few days later. "Don't overspend," he said. "One of my jobs as President is to make sure we keep fiscal sanity in the budget."[20] In this divided government scenario—a Democratic Senate and a GOP House—staring down Congress was essential.

The strategy of the Blade and the Veto Pen seemed to be working. Democrats were beginning to take the threats seriously and started coping with the realization that they might not be able to translate their majority status in the Senate to their advantage on budget issues. "Instead of a long, hot fall, it's over," said Representative Charles Stenholm of Texas. "There'll be no farm bill because there's no money. There'll be no more prescription drug bill."[21]

That was 4 September. Seven days later, the world changed.

In the wake of the 9/11 terrorist attacks, there was naturally a widespread consensus that more money would be spent on defense and homeland security. A $40 billion emergency spending bill was rushed to the president's desk, and Bush stepped back from his original line in the sand on the budget. This time, instead of lodging a veto threat against any bill that spent one penny over his original budget, the president said he would allow $25 billion more in discretionary funding than he had proposed.[22] Daniels told Bush this was a bad idea but Bush ignored his advice.[23]

Suddenly, there was a mad rush to spend more on just about every federal program, whether it was related to defense and homeland security or not. Even some big-spending Democrats realized the dangers in a post-9/11 spending binge. "We have basically opened the door for anything," said Representative

Robert Matsui of California. To provide cover for the budget bloat, the programs were smuggled into defense appropriations bills or dropped into conference reports in the dead of night.

The defense bill was just one of the vehicles for projects that shoveled money to the districts of key Republicans and Democrats. There was $73 million in projects for Senate Appropriations Committee ranking member Ted Stevens of Alaska, including $3.4 million for a landfill in Barrow. A bill funding domestic agencies showered Mississippi—the home state of the Senate's then-minority leader Trent Lott—with more than $16.4 million, including $2.5 million for the National Institute for Undersea Science and Technology at the Stennis Space Center. Pork is a bipartisan phenomenon, of course, and Democrats had a hand in the spending spree, too, resulting in $54 million for Senator Harry Reid's home state of Nevada and over $15 million for the district of Representative Nancy Pelosi of California.[24]

One of the problems with pork projects is that they earmark money in the budgets of various agencies to be used for a specified, usually politically-motivated purpose. Much of the time, it ties up money in operations that are unnecessary or of a low priority and takes away flexibility from the agencies to allocate resources to more important uses, something that is critical when the US is embarking upon an invasion and occupation of a foreign country. For instance, the pork in the defense bill was financed by $2.4 billion taken out of the accounts that supported military training, weapons maintenance, spare parts, and other military "readiness" items.[25] On the occasions when money isn't reallocated from elsewhere to finance the pork, it's simply added to the total cost of government.

All told, Congress piled a record number of 8,341 pork projects (cost: $20 billion) into the bills sent to the president. That was up by around a third from the previous year's record-setting number of projects, and the cost to taxpayers for the pork went up by close to 9%.[26]

As defense expert and former senior analyst for the Senate Appropriations Committee Winslow Wheeler quipped, "War is not hell; it's an opportunity."[27]

Even when Congress wasn't adding new spending, it was taking action to keep other budget cuts from occurring. For instance, Congress postponed a periodic review of excess military base capacity until 2005 to avoid base closures before the elections of 2002 and 2004. The effect was to tie up military spending in operations that even the Pentagon didn't think were essential. Defense Secretary Donald Rumsfeld said of base closure postponement: "What [it] means is that the United States will continue to have something like 20%–25% more bases than we need. We will be spending money . . . that is being wasted to manage and maintain bases we don't need. Given the war on terror, we will be doing something even more egregious, and that is we will be providing force protection on bases that we do not need."[28]

If there were ever a time that Bush could have successfully pulled a "Full Gipper," it was in the wake of the 9/11 attacks. With sky-high approval ratings, he could have done what Reagan did after the attempt on his life: Use the political honeymoon period to call on Congress to make cuts to non-essential programs to pay for the needed increases in military spending. Compelling Congress to forgo the pork projects stuffed into the final bills, for instance, could have offset the entire cost of the emergency appropriation devoted to the war on terror that year.[29] Even a fraction of that restraint would have been worthwhile.

Yet, when the bills finally got to the White House, Bush bailed on the Blade and the Veto Pen strategy. He signed them all into law, even though the bills were much more expensive than the price tag that was supposed to trigger a veto. Instead of killing bills that grew in excess of $25 billion over his proposed budget cap, Bush signed a series of bills that busted the budget by $42 billion. The net result was a one-year 10% increase in discretionary spending after adjusting for inflation—the biggest real rate of growth since 1967, and almost twice what Bush had proposed.

Most of that increase had little or nothing to do with the war on terror. The Congressional Budget Office estimates that the amount of money actually earmarked to the war on terror and the invasion of Afghanistan only amounted to $17 billion that year, less than a quarter of the overall spending hike.[30]

Bush had missed one of the best opportunities he would ever have to show he was serious about restraining spending. His actions amounted to no less than a surrender in the fight against the big spenders of both parties.

There wasn't much left for Mitch Daniels to do for the rest of that year than practically concede defeat. He predicted deficits for the rest of Bush's first term and lamented the inability of federal policymakers to find offsets for new military spending.[31] "Discretionary spending, by the time we are done this year, is going to wind up growing something like 13% (in nominal terms)," said Daniels. "It would be a very serious mistake to let those [kinds] of growth rates—underlying growth rates—continue and pile the guns on top of butter."[32]

The White House still continued to threaten vetoes. In April of 2002, Bush again noted that forthcoming appropriations bills would be viewed with skepticism. "I've got a tool, and that's called a veto," he said.[33] It was fast becoming obvious, however, that Bush wasn't really willing to use that tool, and it appeared as if Congress knew that the rhetoric was hollow.[34]

It was, of course.

Bush did not veto a single bill in his entire first term. That is rare in US history. In fact, no president since John Quincy Adams has served an entire term and not vetoed anything. When it comes to appropriations bills, Bush joins Lyndon Johnson as the only other president of the last seventy years to serve an entire term without vetoing at least one budget bill in his first four years. Every other president found several worth vetoing. Carter vetoed two spending bills that the Democratic Congress sent to him. Nixon vetoed three in his first term, George H.W. Bush vetoed eight, and Reagan vetoed four before he was re-elected in 1984.

Even if Bush vetos bills at any point in the remainder of his second term, it won't be enough to hold the line on a federal budget that is already in overdrive. Bush gave Big Government a four-year head start.

A BITTER HARVEST

We've already seen how the attempt to end farm programs fared. Two years into the mandated phaseout, the GOP majority in Congress doubled farm subsidies and further uprooted its commitment to the slow termination of the subsidies every subsequent year. Between 1998 and 2001, payments to farmers cost taxpayers $63 billion above what they would have cost if Congress had honored its promise.[35]

The Freedom to Farm Act was set to officially expire in 2001. Small-government conservatives were hoping the president could breathe new life into the attempt to wean farmers off the federal teat. In the summer of 2001—months before Bush's capitulation to the big spenders in the fall—there was still some hope. He'd taken a crack at cutting farm subsidies in his first budget, and there were whispers around the Capitol that he would go after them again in his next budget.

Agriculture lobbyists were already grazing the halls of Congress that summer and were ready to stampede once the spending binge that characterized the congressional response to 9/11 began. Farm program supporters are very savvy marketers. They were among of the first to pick up on the trick of hitching their favored programs to the national security bandwagon. They named their newest taxpayer shakedown the Farm Security Act.

Republican congressman Terry Everett of Alabama sent a letter to his colleagues urging them to support the bill in the aftermath of the terrorist attacks. "The bipartisan Farm Security Act provides a strong safety net . . . and strengthens America's national security." Supporting the measure would help "keep America strong," wrote Everett. To GOP senator Richard Lugar of Indiana—a long-time critic of price supports and ranking member of the Senate Agriculture Committee—this was sheer pabulum. "To imply somehow we need a farm bill in order to feed our troops, to defend our nation, is ridiculous."[36]

What the bill would surely do is put the last nail in what was fast becoming an expensive coffin for the Freedom to Farm Act.

It would give $170 billion in taxpayer money to farmers over ten years. It would extend subsidies for a variety of crops like grain, cotton, sugar, wool, and honey. It would lock into place the mohair subsidy that Republicans had killed in 1995 and resurrected in 1998.

The bill would even add a new layer of subsidies on top of the old failed system of price supports, and extend the infrastructure of the farm welfare state to dairy farmers in New England and peanut farmers in Georgia. The peanut lobbyists were, of course, ready with a sound bite aimed at convincing taxpayers that their clients were justified in asking for money. Said Richard Pasco, counsel for the American Peanut Product Manufacturers lobbying group, "The peanut butter and jelly sandwich is as American as apple pie."[37] The comparison was more apt than most people probably realized at the time. Congress had created (and Bush signed into law) a new $95 million subsidy program for apple growers just months before.

One of the biggest myths of federal farm programs is that they are vital to preserving impoverished and beleaguered family farms in the United States. The reality is quite different from the popular notions about farming in America today. Most farmers are relatively wealthy. Average household income for family farms in 2001 was $64,465. That's 10.7% more than the average US household income. By contrast, when large-scale federal farm subsidies began in the 1930s, farmers' incomes were only half the national average.[38] As the Department of Agriculture reported recently, "Farm households have higher incomes, greater wealth, and lower consumption expenditures than do other US households."[39]

Most farmers don't even receive direct subsidies from the federal government. The handouts go to only one-third of the nation's farmers, mainly to large agribusinesses. In 2004, the most recent year for which comprehensive statistics are available, 62% of all subsidies go to only 10% of all recipients.[40]

Many Fortune 500 companies often receive farm welfare checks. Most of the corporate recipients are agricultural or farm-centered corporations (such as Archer Daniels Midland, International Paper, and Tyson Foods). Others, however, are companies most people don't associate with farming, such as Chevron and Texaco. Put all this together and a new reality emerges: Instead of being a program intended to salvage a way of life, farm subsidy programs are actually one of the biggest corporate welfare handouts in the entire federal budget.

By January 2002, however, Mitch Daniels was being directed by the president—despite an earlier vow to cut agriculture programs—to include a huge increase in farm subsidies in the new budget. Daniels objected, but it was useless. The OMB director was backed into a corner. The next thing he knew, he was writing letters to farm-state Republicans reassuring them of the White House's support.[41]

By February 2002, the president was promoting the ridiculous notion that failure to pass a farm bill would jeopardize the security of the national food supply. "This nation has got to eat," Bush told an audience at the Cattleman's Beef Association in Denver. "It's in our national security interests that we be able to feed ourselves."[42]

It was more than enough to alienate fiscal conservatives who were already having their doubts about the president's general commitment to spending discipline. Republican representative Jeff Flake of Arizona complained, "I've been away from the farm for a long time, but I still know manure when it's being shoveled." Ohio Republican John Boehner noted that the farm bill was "a U-turn back to the past. . . . We're going back to what we know didn't work."[43]

The budget hawks in the House, the ranks of which now included members like Flake and Pat Toomey of Pennsylvania, joined the last remaining GOP revolutionaries like John Shadegg to try to slow down the farm bill. They knew there was very little chance they'd be able to defeat the juggernaut, but they were going to try to throw a wrench into its gears anyway. Their best hope was teaming up with Democrats who had concerns with the environmental impact of federal farm programs.

During the debate on the House floor, Pat Toomey railed against the bill, calling it "a step toward Soviet-style agriculture" and warned that it would turn "farmers into dependent serfs of the federal government."[44] The conservatives were defeated by 251 other members of the House—most of them members of their own party—who thought the amendment was a minor annoyance on the path to passage. The conservatives in the Senate weren't having any better luck. Sam Brownback of Kansas, a graduate of the Republican Revolution class, was one of only twenty-eight GOP senators to vote against the bill.

The only bone thrown to the conservatives was a promise from the White House not to hold a high-profile signing ceremony.[45] The discontent with the president coming from conservatives was obvious to Bush's advisers, but it didn't change their mind about signing the bill. Karl Rove, obviously aware that

Bush's embrace of farm programs would severely undermine any future claim to fiscal responsibility, joked that Bush should sign the bill "by candlelight."[46] But sign it he must. There was an election on the line, and buying off the farm lobby was a vital component of Rove's strategy to retake the Senate.

The farm bill debacle left conservative Republicans, often inclined to give the president the benefit of the doubt, very skeptical that he was still on their side—or, for that matter, whether he ever was. The usually optimistic John Shadegg, then-chairman of the Republican Study Committee, was starting to feel that the great Republican victory of 2000 wasn't all that conservatives hoped it would be. "My gut tells me the only conclusion of all of this is it's very hard to change Washington."[47]

Unnamed GOP sources on the Hill lamented to reporters that if Bush signed the farm bill, he would sign anything. Soon conservatives would have undeniable proof of that when the gargantuan Medicare drug benefit barreled down Pennsylvania Avenue.

BAD MEDICINE

In the midterm elections of 2002, the GOP regained control of the Senate by two seats. Thus the stage was set for the GOP to enact the biggest expansion of the welfare state since the Great Society.

Bush placed the prescription drug benefit for Medicare at the top of his to-do list for 2003. He had endorsed the idea of a drug benefit for seniors during the 2000 presidential campaign. To his credit, the initial proposal included some modest but much-needed reform of the program by introducing to the system a form of competition from private-sector insurance providers. The drug benefit component was tailored toward the neediest seniors and was not supposed to be an open-ended entitlement for everyone. And the point wasn't to simply tack on a new benefit for Medicare but to also require the comprehensive reformation of a failing program that was careening to fiscal insolvency. The two were supposed to be inseparable. Some of the reforms were even policy ideas that were part of the GOP gospel during the Republican Revolution.[48]

Once in office, Bush's drug plan became more ambitious and expensive. While the campaign plan might have only cost around $158 billion over ten years, the new Bush plan was supposed to cost $400 billion over ten years—itself a severe and possibly deliberate underestimate, as we'll see. The new Bush plan would cover more seniors and place more of the cost on taxpayers than his campaign plan would, but at least it still included some market-based reform of the system. The political strategy hinged on increasing the amount the government spent on drugs for seniors as a way to grease the skids for the politically more difficult debate on reform.

But before Bush's plan could go anywhere, the White House needed to help the Republicans solve a little problem in the Senate. Incoming majority leader Trent Lott had recently made some bizarre comments at a birthday celebration for Strom Thurmond in December 2002. A little too caught-up in the praise of Thurmond's career, Lott suggested that the nation would have been better off if Thurmond—who ran for president as a segregationist on the Dixiecrat Party ticket—had won the

White House in 1948. The media, spurred mainly by bloggers who broke the story, had a field day with the comments, and it was only a matter of time before Lott had to leave his leadership position to avoid further embarrassment to Republicans. The White House did not immediately abandon Lott, but after a few days of bad press they sent word that it was time to go. There was one condition, however: Senator Bill Frist of Tennessee, the chairman of the National Republican Senatorial Committee, had to be his successor.

Why Frist? Because he was a doctor—a world-renowned heart-transplant surgeon—and obviously a man with supreme credibility on health care issues. But he was also a big supporter of Bush's plan to expand Medicare. Thus the changing of the guard was complete.[49]

Perhaps it's appropriate that one of the first high-level briefings on the Medicare proposal by Frist and House Speaker Dennis Hastert to the top brass from some of the biggest companies in America occurred in the Lyndon Johnson Room of the Senate. The ornate, fresco-ceiling meeting room was still home to the weekly caucus meetings of the Democrats. It even has a portrait of LBJ himself that must have been gazing approvingly upon the proceedings. Frist made sure everyone in the room knew this wasn't just going to be a big increase in spending. There was going to be real reform, too. "When you have a Republican Congress and Republican president . . . you want to be bolder," said the new majority leader.[50]

Bills were moving through the House and Senate simultaneously that summer, but a funny thing happened on the way to the forum. The reform components disappeared.

In the House, the GOP leaders agreed to demands by the more leftish Republicans to delay and severely restrict the competition of private health plans. Instead, the House bill managers—led by Tom DeLay, now the majority leader—agreed to gut the reforms by turning the elements of private competition within the Medicare program into a six-metropolitan-area pilot program. Even that wouldn't begin until 2010 and would only last six years.[51] Thus, five months after it had been proposed, the major reform elements of the plan were abandoned.

A deal like this wasn't inevitable. Why they felt the need to appease the left-wing of the GOP so quickly seems to indicate how eager Republicans were to get a deal—any deal—out the door quickly.

It also indicates how serious the conservative opposition was to the Medicare plan. As John Shadegg, head of the Republican Study Committee, wrote in the *Arizona Republic* on why he could not support the House bill, "Congress is on the verge of imposing a staggering financial burden on our children, pushing Medicare closer to financial collapse and losing a once-in-a-lifetime opportunity for reform."[52] Representative Mike Pence of Indiana told *USA Today*, "The White House and Republican leadership have not accurately calculated the impact of this new federal entitlement on our conservative base."[53]

So, DeLay needed to troll for votes from liberal Republicans to offset the opposition from the conservatives. Bush and the leadership were simply desperate to declare victory on a Medicare bill and were willing to steamroll the conservative Republicans to get it.

Soon White House Press Secretary Ari Fleischer was making

it clear to the press that the president would indeed support *any* bill that came out of Congress.[54] Senate Finance Committee chairman Charles Grassley told reporters that the president had repeatedly signaled his willingness—even as early as the month after the midterm elections—to compromise on the free-market reform elements as long as it got him a drug benefit bill to sign at the end of the day.[55]

Meanwhile, bean counters within the Bush administration were sitting on an accounting bombshell. They realized Congress had cost estimates of the drug program that were too low. The Congressional Budget Office estimated it would cost around $400 billion—that was the amount written into the budget and the amount that members of Congress anticipated would be the ten-year cost of the program. But the actuaries at the Department of Health and Human Services knew the number was more like $534 billion.[56] The chief actuary for Medicare, Richard Foster, was pressured not to release the higher number by his boss, the chief administrator of Medicare, Thomas Scully—a Bush appointee. Scully knew releasing a higher estimate might kill the chances that the bill would pass. So Scully threatened to fire Foster if he released the information. Foster kept his job and his numbers to himself.[57]

Pushing for the drug benefit from outside Congress was Newt Gingrich, who had jumped into the fray to try to help the White House get conservative votes for the bill. He appealed to his former colleagues in the pages of the *Wall Street Journal* and tried to convince them with an argument that boiled down to: An expansion of Medicare is inevitable and possibly even desirable. Republicans might as well get credit for it. If we don't do it, the Democrats will. And their bill will be worse. (Incidentally, Gingrich also fell for the fiction that the bill would cost no more than $400 billion over ten years. In fact, that was part of the appeal of the bill in his eyes and one of the arguments he used to try to sway the conservative opposition.)[58]

As the vote approached, Bush started working the phones. It's not rare for a president to lobby members of Congress on a crucial vote at the last minute. It was odd, however, that Bush was starting so early—ten hours before the floor vote in the House. Political pundits knew what that meant: The Republicans still didn't have enough votes to pass the bill.[59]

One of these calls went to Representative Tom Feeney of Florida. When the president asked him to support the bill, Feeney told him, "I came here to cut entitlements, not grow them."

"Me too, pal," said Bush before he slammed the phone down.[60]

When the vote began, there was plenty of arm-twisting on the House floor, too. Speaker Dennis Hastert, normally one to leave the lobbying to others, was actively involved. So was Health and Human Services secretary Tommy Thompson, even though Cabinet members appearing in the House or Senate chambers during a vote was a break in long-standing courtesy and tradition.[61]

Tom DeLay, however, was in his element. He was the best arm-twister the GOP had. He was nicknamed "the Hammer" for his ability to pound votes out of colleagues and campaign money out of lobbyists and donors.

When he approached Nick Smith of Michigan, DeLay made an offer that could have come from the likes of Tony Soprano.

According to Smith, DeLay told him that in exchange for support of the drug bill, a $100,000 check would be forwarded to the campaign of his son, Brad Smith, who was running to succeed his father in the same House district. The offer, which can really only be construed as a bribe, came with a threat, too: If Smith didn't vote in favor of the bill, GOP donors would boycott his son's campaign.[62] Smith still refused to support the bill. His son ended up losing the Republican primary.

When votes go to the House floor, they usually stay open for fifteen minutes. That wasn't the case this time. The vote was open for three hours. That's how long it took the House leaders to wrangle up enough votes to pass the bill. It was the longest roll call in the modern history of the House.

The Democrats—eager to pass the bill since it would make subsequent expansions of Medicare easier—were being told by minority leader Nancy Pelosi that they could support the bill only after the GOP got all the votes necessary to pass it on their own first. She didn't want the members of her team providing the winning margin on this one. Thus the lobbying of the conservatives became even more intense. The members who had been vocal about their opposition—members of the Republican Study Committee like Flake, Shadegg, Pence, and Trent Franks of Arizona—were bombarded with pleas from the leaders and the president. None of them budged.

Then the House leadership made a fateful decision. They would allow the House version of the bill to fail and then bring up for a vote the even more expensive Senate version of the bill. And the GOP leaders had assurances from the Democrats that they could deliver 200 votes if the Senate version hit the floor.

Conservatives disliked that bill even more than the House version, and this tactic put them in an awkward position.

It also showed how eager the Republican leadership was to get a Medicare drug benefit at all costs. Instead of losing a vote because the conservative members wanted to vote on principle, they resorted to forcing them to decide between the slightly lesser of two very big evils. It was finally enough to scare three Republicans who had initially registered a "nay" to change their vote. Two of them—Trent Franks of Arizona and Ernest Istook of Oklahoma—were members of the RSC.

The GOP finally had the votes, and the gavel dropped immediately. The bill passed 220 to 215. Later, the House version of the bill passed in the Senate by a vote of 54–44.[63]

The vote was a first in many ways, none of them worth bragging about. As congressional expert Norm Ornstein of the American Enterprise Institute noted: "The Medicare prescription drug vote—three hours instead of 15 minutes, hours after a clear majority of the House had signaled its will [in opposition]—was the ugliest and most outrageous breach of standards in the modern history of the House." Ornstein also noted it was a violation of the very principles of legislative discipline that were set down ten years before. "In 1995, soon after the Republicans gained the majority, Speaker Newt Gingrich declared his intention to make sure that votes would consistently be held in the fifteen-minute time frame. The 'regular practice of the House,' he said would be 'a policy of closing electronic votes as soon as possible after the guaranteed period of fifteen minutes.'"[64] The Medicare vote was a breaking of that pledge. Now the Republicans were acting just like the arrogant

Democratic majority they had replaced. Politics had triumphed over principle, again.

The Medicare drug bill was the most terrible defeat for fiscal conservatives yet. For starters, the costs of the program were going to be staggering. The expense of the program continued to go up after the program was enacted, and today one of the most comprehensive estimates suggests it will cost $700 billion over ten years, not $400 billion as originally promised.[65]

After the drug benefit became law, the White House finally released the higher cost estimate that had been bottled up. As the gravity of what they had just done began to dawn on members of Congress, there was a sense of betrayal among many Republicans, especially the fiscal conservatives who trusted the president and voted for the drug benefit despite deep misgivings. The *Washington Post* reported just a few months after the bill was signed into law that discontent over the Medicare bill was high on Capitol Hill. Many members even doubted the bill could pass if it went to a vote again knowing what everyone knows now. Senator Lindsey Graham of South Carolina, former House member during the Republican Revolution and one of the leaders of the opposition to the drug benefit, summed up the sentiments of many of his colleagues: "There is buyers' remorse among many who voted for it."[66]

But the ten-year time frame is too small to show the true costs of the program. The real damage occurs over the lifetime of the benefit. Budget wonks have come up with a concept called "unfunded liability" to describe how big the difference really is between what politicians promised to give seniors and what the government can actually give them, in perpetuity, with the taxes collected for Medicare. The unfunded liability of the Medicare drug benefit over the long term is $18 *trillion*.[67] These numbers are in what economists call "net present value" terms. Cutting away the jargon, what that really means is if the government wanted to pay outright for all these benefits in the future, it would need $18 trillion in a bank account *right now* earning interest. That's a pretty big number. Bigger than the US economy, actually: GDP in 2006 will likely only be in the neighborhood of $13 trillion.

For the first time in twenty-three years, the Republican Party leadership had embraced not just a more expensive government but a markedly more expansive government as well. While Reagan was not able to redefine the boundaries of the welfare state, he at least did not massively expand the role for it. The Republican Revolution was able not only to make government smaller as a percentage of GDP but also to pass landmark welfare reform and, for a time, agricultural reform. The Bush presidency, on the other hand, has produced nothing but substantially larger and more intrusive government so far.

The expansion of Medicare will likely be seen as a turning point in the history of the GOP. It violated all of their principles. It is the biggest expansion in government since the Great Society. And it was passed thanks to the sort of political bullying they once derided. The days of Republican leaders jumping into the breach to lead a crusade to restrain or reduce the cost and scope of government were gone.

The GOP, for all intents and purposes, had become a party of Big Government. Every spending binge before this was just practice. The Medicare drug vote was the coming-out party.

THE ROAD TO HELL, PART II

As soon as Republicans swallowed the bitter pill of the drug benefit, they set their sights on a huge new highway bill. The 2004
bill was going to be even bigger than the $218 billion bill passed
in 1998. That one was loaded with a record number of pork
projects. It would take a little work to beat that record, but
Republican leaders were up for the challenge. House Speaker
Dennis Hastert made the bill one of his top legislative priorities.

Meanwhile, conservatives were pleading with President Bush
to veto something—anything—and the highway bill seemed like
the perfect candidate. The current Senate version would cost $318
billion, and the House version was going to cost $275 billion. The
president made another veto threat and drew the line at $256 bil-
lion. But the veto threats were even more meaningless now.

The mainstream media was starting to catch on to the fact
that Bush's fiscal record was abysmal, too. In February 2004, Tim
Russert of NBC's *Meet the Press,* asked the president about
whether the conservatives had a point when they said his fiscal
record was something to be ashamed of. Instead of admitting
that Republicans should redouble their efforts to get spending
under control, Bush simply denied there was a problem. "Well,
they're wrong," he said.[68]

Conservatives weren't going to rely on the president's veto
threat this time. They were going to try to stall the highway bill
on their own. There were attempts to get Senate majority leader
Frist to delay consideration of the bill, but those attempts were
foiled by Frist himself. The Senate ended up passing their version of the bill in February by a veto-proof majority, prompt-

ing Senator Rick Santorum, who voted against the bill, to quip, "Never get between a congressman and asphalt because you will get run over."[69]

In the House, support of the leadership for an election-year budget-buster was hard to overcome, too. Don Young of Alaska, chairman of the House Transportation and Infrastructure Committee, was already starting to throw money around.[70] Promise him you'd vote for the bill, and you'd get $14 billion to spend.[71]

Representative Jeff Flake tried to slow the bill down by sponsoring an amendment that proposed the infinitely reasonable reform of returning all the money spent on the pork projects directly to the departments of transportation in the state of each earmarked project. That way, the state officials could decide what to do with the money, instead of members of Congress who had little incentive to direct the money to the most effective uses. His amendment became roadkill in a vote of 367 to 60. The House then overwhelmingly passed its version of the bill— $43 billion less than the Senate's but $19 billion more than the president's request.

Then the bill got bottled up in the conference committee tasked with ironing out the differences. The delay had nothing to do with the president's veto threat. Instead, the House and Senate conferees were arguing over how much *more* to spend. The bill was finally put on hold pending the results of the 2004 election.

When the Republicans came back to town in 2005, they had three more seats in the House, four more seats in the Senate, and even less interest in fiscal discipline than when they left town. The highway bill feeding frenzy became more intense, fueled partly by a White House announcement that they would now accept a highway bill over $10 billion bigger than the one they said they would veto last year. Thousands more pork projects were added to the bill. When Jeff Flake and John Shadegg asked Don Young to take the money offered to them for pork and reroute it directly to state officials so they could decide what to do with it, he refused.[72]

The final tally of pork projects grew to over twice as much as the 1998 bill, and the total size of the bill grew on paper to $286 billion. But that number was fiction. An accounting gimmick was hidden inside the final bill that assumes Congress will simply vote not to spend $8.5 billion on 30 September 2009, one day before the bill expires.[73] So the real cost would be $295 billion over six years. That's 35% bigger than the 1998 bill.

True to form, Bush acted as if he'd never issued a veto threat and signed the bill in a highly publicized press op in Speaker Denny Hastert's congressional district that August.[74]

Before the summer congressional break, the GOP leaders issued talking points to members of Congress. They laid out twelve "Ideas for August Recess Events." The ideas ranged from visiting a bridge or highway that will receive additional funding thanks to the highway bill or talking up the new prescription drug benefit. Not a single one of the points had anything to do with the promise of limiting government.[75]

That summer, Senator Tom Coburn of Oklahoma—a fiscal conservative bomb-thrower in the House and one of the Gang of Eleven who had been elected to the Senate on a platform of cutting spending—noted, "You have to be courageous not to spend money, and [the Republicans] don't have many people

who have that courage." Jeff Flake was even less charitable: "If
you look at fiscal conservatism these days, it's in a sorry state.
Republicans don't even pretend anymore."[76]

THE GRAND OLD SPENDING PARTY

How far afield are Republicans from the goal of restraining Big
Government today? Let me count the ways.

In Bush's presidency so far, the federal budget has grown by
27% after the adjusting for inflation. That's more than twice as
fast as during the eight years of President Clinton. Putting things
into more historical context helps us see how truly dismal the
fiscal record of united Republican governance has been. You
can see in the chart (below) how Bush stacks up against presidents over the past forty years: Even after adjusting for inflation
and number of years in office, he's the biggest spender since
Lyndon B. Johnson.[77]

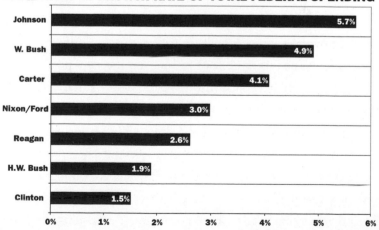

RANKING THE PRESIDENTS:
REAL ANNUAL GROWTH RATE OF TOTAL FEDERAL SPENDING

Johnson	5.7%
W. Bush	4.9%
Carter	4.1%
Nixon/Ford	3.0%
Reagan	2.6%
H.W. Bush	1.9%
Clinton	1.5%

0%   1%   2%   3%   4%   5%   6%

Members of President Bush's staff argue that much of the budget growth has been essential to bolstering the defense of the nation and defending the US against the threat of global terrorism here and abroad. As Joshua Bolten—Mitch Daniels' successor at OMB—wrote in a *Wall Street Journal* op-ed in 2003: "Most critics of the president's fiscal record begin by saying they support the additional spending that has been necessary to respond to 9/11 and the global war on terror, but they then proceed to complain about spending levels that are largely made up of those costs."[78]

Even some critics of the White House make this claim. The Center for Budget and Policy Priorities (CBPP), a left-of-center think tank, suggests that, "[t]he spending growth to date that has resulted from actions policymakers have taken in the past few years has been concentrated primarily in the defense, homeland security, and international affairs areas."[79]

Defenders of the Bush administration also suggest that many of the increases we're seeing now were baked into the cake by Clinton, particularly on the entitlements side of the budget. Some even say that it's wrong to penalize the president for program growth in things like Social Security and Medicare that are on autopilot anyway.

As we've already seen, the president and Congress can add new entitlement programs. They can reduce or eliminate them, too, although they rarely do that. If Republicans were indeed worried about Clinton's stealth budget increases getting out of control, they could have stopped them. It seems quite apparent they didn't want to.

But let's return to Bolten's point. Yes, it is certainly true that other presidents did not have to make room in the budget for programs directed at defending the United States against global terrorism. So let's take defense and homeland security out of the equation. Let's also give Bush and the Republicans the benefit of the doubt and take entitlement spending off the table, too. Yet, they still don't come out looking much better. In fact, they come out looking worse.

Bush pulls ahead of Johnson by this standard, as you can see in the next figure. Nixon and Ford pull into first place because nondefense and non-entitlement spending grew as a share of the budget during that eight year period, while the military budget shrank as a percentage of the whole as the US withdrew from Vietnam.

REAL ANNUAL GROWTH RATE OF FEDERAL SPENDING (MINUS DEFENSE, HOMELAND SECURITY, AND ENTITLEMENTS)

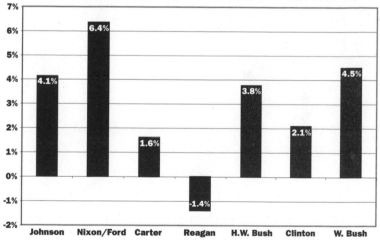

Now take a look at how George W. Bush's annualized rate of budget growth falls. It drops from around 5% in the previous chart to 4.5% in this one. If defense were really driving the budget bloat, this would move downward much more substantially than it actually does.

Once entitlement spending is taken off the table, presidents have two choices of where to allocate money in the budget. As budget watchers used to say, the federal government can either buy guns (by funding defense programs) or butter (by funding nondefense programs). What's remarkable about the George W. Bush years is that he has been spending taxpayer money on guns and butter simultaneously, reversing a trend that has been the norm for all Republican presidents over the past four decades.

During the Cold War, presidents like Ronald Reagan who wanted to increase spending on defense made room for it by cutting nondefense spending (or at least by spending money on those programs at a rate lower than inflation). Presidents who were in office after the end of a war—such as Richard Nixon and Gerald Ford after Vietnam—had the benefit of falling real defense expenditures, which they were more than happy to spend on nondefense programs. Only two Cold War presidents after 1964, Johnson and Carter, presided over real increases in both the defense and nondefense budget.

After the end of the Cold War, presidents found savings in the defense budget as a result of military demobilization upon the collapse of the Soviet Union. This "peace dividend" fueled increases in nondefense programs. While inflation-adjusted defense spending did begin to grow during the latter half of the Clinton administration (primarily under pressure from the Republican majority in Congress), the defense budget was still smaller in real terms at the end of the Clinton presidency than the beginning.[80]

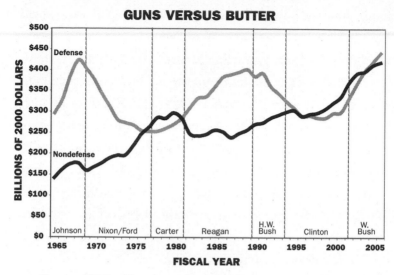

GUNS VERSUS BUTTER

George W. Bush's tenure, however, is a return to the Johnson and Carter philosophy of budgeting: across-the-board increases in everything. Inflation-adjusted defense spending is higher today ($440 billion) than it was at the high point of Reagan's defense buildup ($399.6 billion) and outstrips Johnson's largest Vietnam War defense budget ($421.3 billion). And real non-defense spending has grown by a total of 25% during Bush's presidency so far, compared to 15% over Clinton's entire presidency.

Besides, not every penny in the military budget goes to the war on terror. The Congressional Budget Office estimated that the amount of money in the defense budget that is directed to the (broadly defined) "war on terrorism" (which includes money spent on the invasion, occupation, and rebuilding of Iraq) has equaled $323 billion through January 2006.[81] Spending on the war on terror only amounts to 15% of combined defense spending for the past five years. That leaves 85% of the defense budget going to fund a lower priority. As we've already seen, much of the time those lower priorities are unnecessary weapons systems that remain alive because of congressional whimsy, like the B-2 bomber in the 1990s.

Lots of the growth in the nondefense budget has been in the one hundred largest programs Republicans pledged to eliminate during the Republican Revolution. We've already seen how the GOP wasn't able to terminate most of those programs, and the ones it did exterminate rose from the grave and prospered. They grew by 11% by the end of Clinton's tenure. Under Bush so far, these programs have grown even faster—by 14% in inflation-adjusted terms.

In truth, the *real* big money is not even in all of the defense and nondefense discretionary programs, which only make up about 40% of the federal budget. The remaining 60% is swallowed up by entitlement programs. And here, too, Bush and the Republican Congress look more like Nixon and Johnson than Reagan and Clinton, as you can see in the table on the next page.

Even if Reagan didn't scale back the boundaries of the welfare state, you have to give him credit for holding them to a 2% real annual growth rate. The Republican Revolution's welfare reform helped Clinton's standing in this comparison. But the GOP over the past five years has done next to nothing to restrain entitlement spending, and the growth rates show that. (Incidentally, this chart includes only an estimate for the first year of the Medicare drug benefit. When the costs of that program rise, so will the growth rate, placing the GOP today even more comfortably in the big-spenders category).

These statistics merely show how fast government has grown. To gauge how bad it really is, an obvious question needs to be

REAL ANNUAL GROWTH RATE OF ENTITLEMENT SPENDING

Johnson	8.9%
Nixon/Ford	9.9%
Carter	4.1%
Reagan	2.0%
G.H.W. Bush	4.8%
Clinton	3.3%
G.W. Bush*	5.1%

*Through FY 2006

asked: Compared to what? One of the best ways to show how dramatic these spending increases really are is to compare how big the government has gotten in relation to the overall US economy as measured by gross domestic product, or GDP. This will illustrate how much of the economy is eaten up by government spending.

When the Republicans took control of Congress, government swallowed 20.7% of GDP. When Clinton left office, federal outlays equaled only 18.4% of GDP. That's the lowest government spending had been since 1961. But this trend was reversed almost immediately after George W. Bush's inaugural parade. Together Bush and a Republican Congress managed to expand government spending to 20.8% of GDP in 2006. By this standard, they have effectively overturned the Republican Revolution.

Some have criticized the budget deficits that have appeared under Bush. While many of the critics focus on the tax cuts as the primary cause of these deficits, the truth is much more complex. The economy was slowing down before the tax cut was even enacted. With less economic activity to tax, federal tax revenues would have gone down anyway.

For the sake of argument, let's assume the worst case scenario and say that every dollar of revenue loss was a result of the tax cut. During the first two years of the Bush administration, revenue declined by $206 billion. Spending during that period went up by $297 billion. During that same two-year period, the budget went from a surplus of $128 billion to a deficit of $377 billion, an absolute shift of about $506 billion.[82] Looking at the amount of the spending increase, you notice that it accounts for about 60% of the change. In other words, spending was more responsible for the deficit than the tax cut or the weak economic conditions.

Congress and the president do not really have direct control over how much revenue the government will collect. They do, however, have direct control over how much the government will spend. By definition, deficits are chiefly the result of too much spending.

But all of this is a relatively small ball game in terms of the fiscal imbalance over the long term. What the current deficit numbers don't show is the cost to future taxpayers as a result of permanent expansions in government spending. Those are un-funded liabilities mentioned before. The "deficit" of the Medicare drug benefit is at least $18 trillion in perpetuity. That's the big deficit Bush critics should be worried about.

Simply put, the Bush years have been an awful setback for the cause of limited government.

THE BATTLE AHEAD

Add it all up and it equals heartburn for the fiscal conservatives who had fought so hard to restrain spending. By the summer of

2005, many fiscal conservatives in Congress had finally had it with the GOP leadership. And the feeling was mutual.

Aides to the Republican leaders began to whisper to the press that the members who led the charge against the Medicare bill could expect to remain on the back bench for a long time. Their antagonism toward the highway bill didn't help, either. But it didn't matter. Playing nice with the GOP leaders wasn't the goal of the fiscal conservatives anymore. Big Government had always been their target. And now that the Republican congressional leaders and the president were cogs in the Big Government machine, they too were now targets.

Representative Jeb Hensarling of Texas, one of the rising stars of the conservative movement, said it best when he noted that the events of the first Bush term were "the start of a battle, not the end of one."[83] That battle will have dramatic consequences for the future of the Republican Party.

THE FLAWS
OF BIG GOVERNMENT
CONSERVATISM

Why the Bush Strategy Failed

I n retrospect, everything seems inevitable.

Maybe we should have known that George W. Bush, if elected president, would not embark upon a crusade to limit government. He was all but screaming it at us during the presidential campaign. He proposed $3.6 billion to build community health centers.[1] He hawked a $5 billion plan to improve reading skills of low-income children.[2] He promised a $67 billion "medical moonshot" in federal disease research over the next decade.[3] The National Taxpayers Union tallied up the Bush wish list in 2000 and found it would expand government by around $75 billion annually.[4]

The Republican platform of 2000—a document that usually reflects the preferences of the presidential candidate on key policy issues since it is written almost entirely by campaign operatives—did not include a single reference to eliminating any Cabinet agencies, terminating any federal programs, or controlling the growth of the budget. That's the first time a Republican platform has been mute on the subject in over twenty years. Even Bush's father, no fiscal conservative, called for a freeze on some categories of federal spending in his platform, albeit a "flexible freeze." When George W. Bush claimed he was running as a different sort of Republican, he wasn't kidding.

So why didn't so many conservatives see the era of super-sized government coming?

Maybe it's because while Bush was making grand pronouncements about all the new government programs he wanted to create, his campaign staff was peppering the message with hints about the importance of budget restraint. Campaign spokesman Ari Fleischer tried to assuage the uneasiness among fiscal conservatives by suggesting that a Republican president paired with a GOP Congress would finally be able to do what a GOP House and Senate could not do on their own. "It will take a new president to change the way Washington does business and turn things around," said Fleischer.[5] Economic advisor Lawrence Lindsey told the *Wall Street Journal* that "until we have a president who represents all the people and is willing to say no to additional spending, we have a problem."[6]

Political choices are relative, of course. The Democratic nominee, VP Al Gore, was proposing annual spending increases that were three times larger than Bush's. At least Bush had the advantage of being a Republican, and Republicans—even fiscally conservative ones—wanted to take back the White House. The necessary condition to making some headway against Big Government, they thought, was united GOP control of both ends of Pennsylvania Avenue. The details could be sorted out later.

As Peggy Noonan, former speechwriter for Ronald Reagan, wrote in her on-line *Wall Street Journal* column in 2006: "I didn't understand Mr. Bush's grand passion to be cutting spending. He didn't present himself that way. But he did present himself as a conservative, with all that entails and suggests."[7] And if conservatives stand for anything, it's against Big Government. Yet now that we're five-and-a-half years into Bush's presidency, we've seen an average increase of $169 billion in spending annually instead of the $74 billion annually that was proposed on the campaign trail. Almost two-thirds of that had nothing to do with the war on terrorism.

Bush calls himself a "compassionate conservative" and has uttered the phrase numerous times as if sheer repetition will eventually turn it into a robust political philosophy. Bush-friendly journalist Fred Barnes came up with a more accurate description of Bush's philosophy: Big Government conservatism. Barnes wasn't using the description as an insult, though. In his eyes, and in the eyes of many Bush supporters, this form of conservatism is the wave of the future. It represents an ideological shift that partially explains how the Republicans became the party of Big Government.

THE CONSCIENCE OF A COMPASSIONATE CONSERVATIVE

One of the earliest descriptions of what came to be known as "compassionate conservatism" appeared in a *Washington Post* column in 1997 by David Brooks, then senior editor at the *Weekly Standard* and now a columnist for the *New York Times*. Today, he is a staunch defender of Bush against attacks that the president is severely hurting the cause of limited government.

In the *Post* column, Brooks unearthed a new Republican approach to managing the welfare state. At the time, he called it the "compassion shtick."[8] Simply limiting government was not enough, apparently. Key Republicans—some of whom had started what they called a Renewal Alliance caucus—thought the GOP needed to show a little more soul.

The approach seemed more like an attempt to solve a perceived image problem for Republicans than a wholesale reappraisal of fiscal conservative doctrine. Yet it surrendered to the premise that simply making an overweening, busybody government smaller and less powerful was an act of meanness. So the entire idea of compassionate conservatism has its roots in the concession that the small-government conservative agenda of allowing people to have more control over their own lives— something that, by definition, occurs when you reduce the scope of government—was not in itself a compassionate act.

The goal, however, was not just to remove the government-constructed impediments to the advancement of poor families, but to use government as a tool to help them advance. As then-senator Dan Coats of Indiana explained in an op-ed co-authored with John Kasich for the *Washington Times*, "The fact that government programs have not worked is no excuse for those in government not to act."[9]

This compulsion to actively use government in the service of what were considered conservative goals would eventually become the predicate for a more active government generally under Bush. The philosophy was best summed up in Bush's commandment from a Labor Day speech in 2003: "[W]hen somebody hurts, government has got to move."[10] As one of Bush's first-term speechwriters, David Frum, described it, the principles of the president's actions weren't important. For Bush, "getting things done *was* a principle."[11] This sort of approach was based mainly upon a fantasy of benign government action where the federal government could do good with little or no adverse side effects. It's what motivated Bush to often observe to White House staffers that if the government could ever write a law that could make people love their neighbor, he'd be glad to sign it.[12]

But let's cut back to the Republican flirtation with this theme in 1997 for a minute. The way this newfound form of compassion originally manifested itself was by recommitting the GOP to some fairly standard Republican policies. The difference is that they would be repackaged and dressed up in the language of compassion.

Federal help in reviving civil society, for instance, would take the form of larger tax deductions for charitable contributions. The per-child tax credits like the one that eventually made it into the 1997 budget deal would appeal to those worried about the future of the nuclear family. Also to be repackaged as part of the agenda was the idea of school vouchers, designed to give poor families control over where their child went to school while simultaneously introducing some competition into a stagnant monopoly school system. This was all mainstream GOP fare in 1997. What's more, at least in the case of school vouchers, is that these were ideas that had decades of support from limited-government conservatives.

There was nothing inherent in the strategy that implied the federal government would have to grow, either. These weren't new ideas geared to expanding old government programs or creating new ones just to help people. These policies were originally aimed at slowly extracting the federal government's nose from people's business and letting them have more control over their money and their lives.

Something happened between 1997 and the presidential campaign of George W. Bush. That something was the budget surplus. Suddenly, this new version of conservatism became a philosophy fit for the times. There was no more need to be frugal. As long as there was plenty of money to spend—and there was—Republicans couldn't see a reason to avoid calls for more social spending as long as it went to the right people, the right programs, and Republicans were making the decisions.

Enter the newfound interest in what was still, for lack of a better term, called compassionate conservatism. It helps explain, for instance, the quick Republican capitulation to Clinton's proposal to spend billions of dollars more on hiring new teachers in 1998. Instead of making the case they might have made in years past that education should be a strictly state and local function, they simply let Clinton have the money—as long as local school districts had some sort of flexibility over how to allocate it. Republicans were still afraid of looking mean if they didn't increase spending on schools and teachers to atone for ever daring to terminate the intrusive federal presence in education.

It was only a matter of time before the ideals of compassionate conservative policy—to the extent that it was now distinguishable as a philosophy instead of merely a tactical digression from garden-variety conservatism—morphed into plain old cheerleading for Big Government. Education policy is probably the best example of how it all went wrong. As Major Garrett of Fox News has written: "The story of the education revolution is a three-part story: the utter failure of grand proclamations about destroying the federal education bureaucracy; capitulation to Clinton standpatism . . . and, finally, a reluctant embrace of an intrusive federal mandate [the No Child Left Behind Act] tied to the largest increases in federal education spending in history. There is no part of domestic policy on which congressional Republicans have ended up farther away from where they started. None."[13]

Garrett might have been a bit too kind in saying that Republicans were generally reluctant to pass Bush's education plan. Only about thirty House members concerned about the drastically expanded federal role in education voted against the bill.[14] Many of them were the same conservatives who had been fighting valiantly, but to little avail, against the GOP leaders seemingly hell-bent on destroying the image of the Republican Party as the defenders of small government throughout the late 1990s.

But a large share of both House and Senate Republicans happily voted for the No Child Left Behind Act. Senator Bill Frist, for instance, was an early supporter of the idea. He was also the co-chairman of the campaign committee that removed the perennial call to abolish the Department of Education from the GOP platform during the 2000 presidential campaign. Frist reminded reporters of what the newly compassionate GOP was really all about. Seeking to eliminate federal education programs might lead voters to think "we don't care about education," said the future Senate majority leader. "And if there's one thing Republicans care about, it's kids."[15]

Bush made it clear upon being inaugurated that he would preside over a Republican Party no longer interested in getting the federal government out of the education business. "Change will not come by disdaining or dismantling the federal role in education," he said.[16] But it's not at all clear that Bush ever understood the limited-government conservatives' argument in favor of scaling back the federal role in education in the first place. When interviewed by Fred Barnes in 2005, Bush explained why his strategy is preferable to the one conservatives embarked upon in 1995 and 1996. "We [in the Bush White House] said public schools are important, they've been really important throughout history, let's make them better, as opposed to saying let's abolish them."[17]

Bear in mind that Republicans never advocated abolishing public schools. And eliminating the Department of Education would not result in the closing of a single state or local school anywhere in the country. Bush's inability or unwillingness to distinguish between state and local schools, and the overbearing federal agency that fusses with them, speaks volumes about his view of the world.

Bush promised conservatives there would be market-based reform elements in his education plan. But those elements were weakened before the bill reached Capitol Hill and were practically eliminated altogether once the bill went through the legislative process. By the end, there was almost nothing about the bill that would have been called conservative just years earlier. Instead of trying to default to the only slightly more defensible GOP fallback position of spending more money on the condition that there were as few strings attached as possible, the bill included all sorts of brand new mandates on local schools.

So, just as they would with the Medicare drug benefit two years later, the Republicans successfully expanded government without even getting the benefit of fundamental reforms that limited-government conservatives were promised.[18] By 2006, the Department of Education budget had doubled in inflation-adjusted dollars under Bush, amounting to the largest increase in education spending since Lyndon Johnson.

The theme of the Bush years would *not* be decentralization, the idea that many federal programs could be spun off and block-granted to state and local governments the way they were in the welfare reform legislation. Decentralization relies upon the notion that there are distinct roles for the different levels of government to play. The national government is best suited to handle the really big national ones, like defense, while state and local governments are the best to handle the provision of schools and local roads, for instance.

This used to be a highly-regarded principle in GOP circles going back further than Goldwater. In *The Conscience of a Conservative*, Goldwater makes it very clear that it is one of the main principles of limited government. The Constitution, he notes, "draws a sharp and clear line between federal jurisdiction and state jurisdiction. The federal government's failure to recognize that line has been a crushing blow to the principle of limited government." In Bush's Republican Party, however, decentralization of government power is seen as nothing more than a quaint suggestion. Instead, the bias is to turn every policy question into a federal issue. That alone makes it a fundamentally different approach than the limited-government conservatism of Ronald Reagan and Barry Goldwater.

This can be seen in how much the federal government spends in grants-in-aid to states and localities. These funds generally go to programs that either the federal government forces on the states or that should be funded entirely by the states. Reagan was able to hack away at the amount spent on state grant programs.

By the end of his presidency, spending on them was down by almost 10% in real terms. Growth was kept to 18% between 1994 and 2000 after adjusting for inflation and netting out the grants sent to the states as a result of welfare reform. Under Bush, the growth has been 26% so far. Very little of that increase had to do with spending on homeland security, which only accounts for 3% of grants in 2006.[19]

THE FOLLY OF
BIG GOVERNMENT CONSERVATISM

In a *Wall Street Journal* op-ed published three years into Bush's first term, Fred Barnes noted he preferred the term "Big Government conservative" to describe Bush's governing philosophy.[20] In the essay, Barnes makes it clear that Bush shouldn't be seen as an heir to Reagan on budget matters. "Reagan was a small government conservative who declared in his inauguration address that government was the problem, not the solution. There, Bush begs to differ." This was hardly news to most fiscal conservatives in the summer of 2003.

The label of Big Government conservative "makes them sound as if they aren't conservatives at all," writes Barnes elsewhere in the piece. "But they are. They simply believe in using what would normally be seen as liberal means—activist government—for conservative ends. And they're willing to spend more and increase the size of government in the process." Yet one of the core inclinations of modern limited-government conservatives is a healthy skepticism of power, particularly government power. Big Government conservatism might as well be another

name for modern Big Government liberalism where the ends justify the means. Simply hanging the conservative label on activist
government shouldn't make it more palatable to supporters of
limited government. Barnes' entire defense of Bush veers close to
being an exercise in semantics. It also looks a bit too much like
an after-the-fact rationalization of Bush's policies instead of a
defense of a coherent before-the-fact philosophy.

According to Barnes, however, Bush's new form of conservatism really *should* be, all labels aside, more palatable to supporters of limited government. That's because Bush's end goal is
not to increase the size of government, he says. The budget bloat
is merely a way to buy off the political opposition in order to get
what conservatives really want—market-based reforms of government programs that will, in the long-run, decrease the
demand for government.

As Barnes writes in his book, *Rebel-in-Chief,* "Bush and his
aides have embraced an insight lost on some other conservatives: What matters is not how big government is but what it
does . . . Bush realized that a conservative president can use government policies to expand personal freedom, a conservative
virtue. His reforms to create voluntary investment accounts in
Social Security and health savings accounts in Medicare aim to
do just that."[21]

David Brooks backs Barnes up on the general point. In a *New
York Times* op-ed from 23 October 2005 titled "The Savior of the
Right," Brooks lambastes conservatives for criticizing Bush's budget
record and suggests that as a result of this new strategy, "Bush
hasn't abandoned conservatism; he's modernized and saved it."[22]

The first controversial notion here is that the size of

government doesn't matter. That's automatically something many small-government conservatives would take umbrage with, and rightly so. There's a moral argument to be made in defense of smaller government. Every increase in the size of government beyond a few core functions does, by definition, translate into a decrease in personal liberty in some way.

The economic impact of Big Government cannot be ignored, either. Over the past decade, numerous economic studies have shown that when the government grows as a share of GDP, the nation is worse off than it would be otherwise. Browsing the academic literature on the subject, you find that growth in government generally stunts economic growth.[23]

None of the academic studies imply that government growth will stop the economy from expanding altogether, of course. They simply show that the economy will grow more slowly than it ought to. It's like the difference between how fast you can hike up a mountain carrying only your own sleeping bag compared to how fast you can climb when you have to haul the entire campsite. Simply put, increased government spending puts a burden on the economy. Lowering government spending would remove that burden.

The authors of the academic studies—and, for that matter, most limited-government conservatives—don't think that all government spending is bad, either. There needs to be some sort of expenditure on law enforcement and defense, for instance, but the federal government spends money on far more than just those essential functions. A report for the Joint Economic Committee of Congress notes: "As [the federal government] moves beyond [its] core functions, the tax and spending policies of government soon become counterproductive and they begin to restrain economic growth and cause income levels to fall well below their potential. This is precisely what has happened in the United States and other [developed] countries in recent decades."[24] This is another reason why limited-government conservatives are worried about the cost of government—it also indicates a much broader scope for government.

So, what's the magic number? Is there a level below which the restraints of government are loose enough to keep potential economic growth from suffocating, and yet still provide a stable environment for the marketplace to thrive? The data suggests there is. "All of the evidence," concludes the Joint Economic Committee study, "suggests that the level of government that maximizes the performance of the economy would place government expenditures at 15% or less of GDP."

Fifteen percent. That's actually pretty generous when you consider that the money spent on all the functions of government explicitly enumerated in the US Constitution only equals around 10% of GDP.[25] And recall that under President Clinton and a Republican Congress, government spending was on a glide path to 15% of GDP. If the federal budget had grown from the day George W. Bush was inaugurated at the same annual rate it had for the six years before he came to office, the federal government would consume only 17% of GDP today. That would be the smallest the federal government has been since the 1950s. Instead, the size of government is around 20% of GDP today. The difference amounts to over $1,300 for each man, woman, and child in America. Or, to put it another way, an average of $4,300 for each taxpayer.

But let's give Barnes the benefit of the doubt and say that the current size of government doesn't matter. What Bush is trying to do, he says, is shrink government over the long term by pairing budget increases with reforms to wean people off dependency on government benefits. The vehicles for that are personal savings accounts for younger workers trapped in the soon-to-be-bankrupt Social Security and Medicare programs. These accounts will allow participants to accumulate assets that would be used to pay for retirement and health care expenses.

This is hardly a new idea. It's a good one, though. The intellectual case for just this sort of market-driven reform has been constructed by small-government think-tanks during a period of close to three decades, and some of these reforms have been implemented and been phenomenally successful in other countries. Bush did decide to make them a central element in his strategy, and that is one of the few truly bright spots of his presidency.

The major downside, however, is that Bush's grand political strategy hasn't worked. What Barnes suggests is a political winner—coupling the reform with an increase in spending to make the package palatable to all ideological persuasions—has backfired. What we've ended up with instead is more government and no reform to speak of.

The Medicare drug bill is again a perfect example of this. The reform elements, some of which had been proposed years before by the 1994 GOP revolutionaries, were decimated in the final bill. Bush signed it anyway instead of sending it back to Congress and forcing them to send him a more reform-oriented bill.

The one element of reform that did squeak by was an expansion of health savings accounts (or HSAs). These accounts would allow people to have more control over their health care through privately-funded accounts that they own and use for health care expenses. Bush defenders point to this as something that has the potential to get people used to taking more responsibility for their health care decisions and, over time, lessen the demand for government-provided health care benefits, particularly in the retirement years. They are right in that respect. But an expansion of HSAs could have been accomplished without adding a brand new and expensive drug benefit to Medicare. Proposals to expand HSAs have passed the House time and time again, and usually command a majority (albeit a slim one) in the Senate.

The outlook isn't any better for the other components of Bush's reform agenda. Many pundits have argued that Bush handled terribly the campaign for personal-accounts reform of the Social Security system, one of the centerpieces of his second-term agenda.[26] Some have even argued that Bush's concessions to the big spenders sapped his credibility and squandered his political capital, particularly on expanding Medicare, making it impossible to put forward a workable coalition to pass Social Security reform.[27] What we're stuck with instead are the huge costs brought upon by the failure of the Big Government conservative strategy.

Even when he's not finding new ways to expand the role of the federal government, Bush actively uses government to advance what he calls "conservative goals." But that's hardly a triumph for limited-government conservatism, either. A potent conservative critique of Republicans is that they are too eager to use government to their own ends. Just take a look at corporate welfare programs for examples of GOP largesse.

Limited-government conservatives, however, are distinctly

different from social conservatives in that they usually see the expansion of government power as harmful, even if it is in the service of well-meaning ends. They realize government action is always accompanied by unintended consequences.

Take the faith-based initiative program, for instance. Bush has expanded the share of federal money available to faith-based institutions to fund their charitable work. Conservatives for decades have pointed out that private charities are a vital part of civil society and are much better at helping people rise out of poverty than a government program. That's because the private charity measures its success by how many people no longer need their services. Government administrators, on the other hand, measure their success by how big their agencies' budgets are and how many people *still* need their help.

What Bush and other Big Government conservatives have done, however, is make an unjustified leap in logic. Private charities are effective and government programs are not. Ergo, a better federal policy would be to take the money that would have gone to government welfare programs and redirect it to private charities instead. But this overlooks one big problem. What made these charities successful in the first place was the fact that they were completely private. Accepting government money now places a whole new set of restrictions on their operations, resulting in less flexibility for the charity.

This also encourages these charities to lobby for more money, and because they only have finite resources, this shifts their priorities and diverts at least part of their focus from the main goal of helping people. As Ed Gotgart, president of the Massachusetts Association of Nonprofit Schools and Colleges has noted, federal money "becomes almost like heroin. You build your program around the assumption that you can't survive without [it]."[28] Simply put, government funding of private charities is likely to make them less effective than they would be in the absence of the government funding.

Perhaps it's ironic that one of the earliest predictions of how this approach could go wrong came from the person who would later be one of the staunchest supporters of Big Government conservatism, David Brooks. In his original 1997 *Washington Post* op-ed, he wrote, "Conservatives are supposed to be able to distinguish between the private realm and the public. They're supposed to recognize that the public can corrupt the private when it tramples into its sphere."[29]

So what has been the outcome of Big Government conservatism's failed gambit?

A bigger government than we would have had if Republicans had simply chosen to recommit themselves to the battles conservatives knew needed fighting. Even if the GOP wants to now recommit itself to limiting government and fighting for all sorts of spending cuts that commitment entails, its job has been made tougher by the new bigger government made possible by Bush's actions. President Bush's policies will make any subsequent attempts to restrain spending that much harder. In that context, Big Government conservatism and George W. Bush's adherence to it has set back the cause of limited government supporters by many years.

At the end of his book, Barnes opts for the phrase "strong-government conservatism" as a more apt description of Bush's philosophy. But that actually seems like a worse fit than Big

Government conservative. After all, if the government expands as it has under Bush, many of the proper functions of government get waylaid by all other sorts of priorities. This over-extension of scope leads instead to a government that is no longer focused or strong enough to carry out its core functions effectively. As Peggy Noonan has noted: "Money is power, more money for the government is more power for the government. More power for the government will allow it to, among many other things, amuse itself by putting its fingers in a million pies, and stop performing its essential functions well, and get dizzily distracted by nonessentials, and muck up everything. Which is more or less where we are."[30] It is those dizzying distractions that have already begun to destroy Big Government conservatism as a workable political strategy.

THE CURRENCY OF CORRUPTION

Jonathan Rauch, columnist for the *National Journal*, elucidated the change in the Republican governing strategy that occurred shortly before George W. Bush won the presidency. Trying to tame Big Government became secondary to building a strong political machine and a permanent Republican majority. Then, only when they were safely entrenched would the GOP get down to the business of finally reducing the size of the federal behemoth.[31]

When viewed in this context, all of the major expansions in government under Bush—the highway bill, the farm bill, and the Medicare bill—suddenly look like attempts to appeal to various special interest constituencies as part of the GOP machine-building effort. Bush's closest political advisor, Karl Rove, did encourage the president to sign the farm bill for blatantly political reasons. The highway bill is always drenched in politics. And presidential speechwriter David Frum confirms that Rove was behind the purposely leftward drift of the education bill for the purposes of neutralizing political opposition from the teachers' unions.[32]

The foreman of the machine-building project was House Majority Leader Tom DeLay, a.k.a. "The Hammer." The idea was to put K Street—the power corridor in downtown DC that is home to the city's high-end lobbying firms—in cahoots with Republicans to build an entrenched GOP majority. DeLay maintained a list that grouped lobbyists into two categories: "Friendly" and "Unfriendly." Those marked "Friendly" were those who had given generously to the campaigns of GOP candidates. Whenever a lobbyist would come calling, DeLay would leaf through the list to determine what kind of reception his guest would receive.[33] It was during this time that DeLay started a fruitful working relationship with a lobbyist named Jack Abramoff, who eventually gave millions of dollars to GOP political actions committees and persuaded his clients to give millions more.

Lobbying is not an inherently bad thing, of course. All citizens have a right to petition their government. But the nature of Big Government changes the incentives of lobbyists just as it changes the incentives of congressmen. A constitutionally-bounded government is one that taxes everyone to provide public goods for the benefit for all, such as a national defense or a court system. Big Government, on the other hand, is untrammeled by that musty old Constitution and encourages Congress to tax everyone to pay for goods that benefit specific people and groups. This puts lobbyists in a unique position to profit from the redistribution of wealth and power that is the main industry in Washington DC today. And congressmen are often all too happy to oblige.

One of the primary means by which Congress curries favor with K Street is through appropriations "earmarks." Those are the pork projects that litter the stories told in this book. Many earmarks are often placed into bills in the dead of night. Others are smuggled into the bill at the last minute, and the public doesn't even know they are there until after the bill has passed. None of them are subject to congressional debate. Earmarks have been used for decades as a means to garner support from wavering congressmen for various pieces of legislation like the highway bill, but they are also used to reward particular supporters or interest groups. Those groups or their lobbyists, grateful for a government contract or a special favor, often make generous contributions to a particular GOP coffer in return.

The GOP machine-building strategy was part of what led to the huge increase in earmarks since the Republican takeover of Congress. In fact, Republicans have become more promiscuous in the use of earmarks than the Democrats ever were. In the last Democratic Congress, the number of earmarks stood at 1,439. The GOP was able to strip that down to 958 their first year in the majority. Today, however, the number has ballooned to over 15,000.[34] Jeff Flake of Arizona, a leading critic of earmarks, calls them "the currency of corruption."

Lobbyist Jack Abramoff—a man who certainly knew what he was talking about—once called the Appropriations Committee, the birthplace of most earmarks, a "favor factory." Meaty examples abound. Representative Joe Knollenberg of Michigan inserted an earmark into a bill to force Amtrak to haul freight for a business owned by one of his campaign contributors.[35] Representative John Doolittle of California helped steer defense funding totaling $37 million to a California company whose officials and lobbyists helped raise money for Doolittle and his PAC.[36] House Appropriations chairman Jerry Lewis of California funneled millions of dollars in earmarks to the clients of one of his biggest fundraisers.[37]

None of these particular actions is inherently illegal, but they create an overall appearance of impropriety and a definite sense that Republicans are too intoxicated with power and too busy allocating taxpayer-funded spoils to have time for reform of the federal government. This is not a false impression, either. The staffs of many congressmen spend much of their time pursuing earmarks, and this causes them to neglect many of their other duties.[38]

The use of earmarks encourages the overall growth of government, too. Sure, the dollar amounts attached to the earmarks are a small share of the overall appropriations bills every year. At last count they equaled 4.5% of federal money appropriated in 2006.[39] Earmarks, however, have been called the "gateway drug" of the big spending addiction. Once you get a taste, you're hooked. That gives the congressional leaders an ability to gather support for bills that might not otherwise pass, just by tacking on a host of earmarks for key members. A congressman wooed by earmarks is never as vigilant about what's in the other parts of the bill as long as his projects stay intact.

The leaders of the Republican Party in the House and the

Senate are also addicted to earmarks, and this contributes to an overall culture of fiscal irresponsibility that starts at the top. Speaker Dennis Hastert sets the standard on the House side. He's one of the most effective porkbarrelers in Congress. This addiction to earmarks saps the leadership's credibility on matters of fiscal discipline.

Historians might look back on 28 November 2005 as the beginning of the end for Big Government conservatism. That's the day when Representative Randy "Duke" Cunningham of California confessed to taking bribes in exchange for promises of earmarks, and resigned from Congress. He eventually received a jail sentence of eight years and four months. In January 2006, Jack Abramoff pled guilty to conspiracy and fraud charges stemming principally from his lobbying efforts on behalf of Indian tribes. While these two cases are not typical—most lobbyists don't engage in criminal activity and most congressmen don't solicit bribes as Cunningham did—they have had the effect of spurring the media and voters to cast a skeptical eye on the machine the Republicans have built.

In political terms, the use of earmarks has severely weakened the credibility of the Republican Party to claim they are the party committed to reform of Big Government. It makes them look even more like the Democrats they replaced in 1994. After all, House Speaker Jim Wright—one of the poster-boys in the GOP's campaign to show how arrogant and corrupt the Democratic Congress had become by the 1990s—was brought down partly as a result of a $30 million earmark awarded to a dubious development project of a business partner and political contributor.[40] Just as the ethical lapses of the Democrats were a potent campaign issue for Republicans in 1994, the fiscal improprieties of Republicans are likely to be a potent campaign issue in many House and Senate races over the next few years.

Cutting government spending now runs contrary to Republican political aims. Today the GOP is so closely aligned with the mechanisms of Big Government that it finds itself unable and unwilling to shut the contraption down. They have become cogs in the federal government's growth machine. Seen in this context, the corruption scandals that have afflicted the Republican Party over the past year are not just a product of unethical congressmen. They are mainly a natural by-product of the GOP leadership's conscious decisions to give up the fight to limit government.

THE CURSE OF
INCUMBENCY

*How Big Government
Assimilated the Republicans*

Washington DC has always reminded me of a high school. It's cliquish and thrives on popularity contests. And Congress always reminds me of a student government that wastes everyone's time and money. There's one crucial difference, of course. Congress has a lot more money to play with than any student government. Yet they are similar in that, just like a student government, what Congress really needs is some adult supervision. That's usually the president's job, but President Bush seems neither capable of nor interested in providing it.

When pondering why the Republicans became a party of Big Government, I'm reminded of the age-old debate about child rearing: What is more important to the development of habits and behaviors—a child's inherent nature or the specific sort of environment he or she is reared and nurtured in by the parent? Most experts think it's a combination of both, with nature meaning more in some circumstances and nurture meaning more in others.

I think you can explain why members of Congress act the way they do over the span of their time in Washington with the same nature-versus-nurture framework. There are some people who are elected to Congress with a natural inclination to expand government. There are other people elected with a natural inclination to cut spending. But over time, it's the environment—the culture that surrounds members of Congress—that makes the crucial difference. The conditioning received in the congressional environment often turns those who start out with a hope of cutting the budget into some of the biggest spenders of them all. This, too, helps explain how the GOP became a party of Big Government.

THE CULTURE OF SPENDING

Political scientist James Payne used the phrase "culture of spending" to describe the environment in which members of Congress operate during their time on Capitol Hill.[1] While researching a book on the subject, Payne did something many political scientists never do: He took a peek into the world of the congressman to determine how Congress really works. Payne discovered, perhaps not surprisingly, that the average member of Congress works and plays in a world dominated by advocates for Big Government. They are bombarded with pro-spending messages at every turn. They rarely hear from the taxpayers. When they do hear from a taxpayer or a group that represents taxpayers, the complaints are rarely loud enough to break through the cocoon of noise created by the swarms of special interest groups defending their pet programs.

Why? It's simple arithmetic.

Imagine the incentives of the recipients of much of the government largesse compared to the incentives of those who are paying the bills, the taxpayers. Think about, for example, the

National Endowment for the Arts. The grants budget of this program is $47.4 million.[2] That's about 0.01% of income taxes.[3] Now imagine the calculation from the point of view of an average NEA grant recipient. The NEA awarded 1,970 grants in 2004, and the average grant that year was $24,000. A single artist, museum, or theater might have gotten more or less than this, but in any case you can see how much more a grant recipient has at stake than you do as a taxpayer.

So, while the elimination of the NEA would likely only get you back much less than a penny of every dollar you paid in income taxes, the average grant recipient would lose the entire $24,000. The grant recipient has a substantially larger incentive to get the attention of Congress—by hiring a lobbyist, testifying in front of a committee, and otherwise trying to influence the decisions of policymakers—than you do as a lone taxpayer.

That's just a small government program. Let's consider a bigger program I've already mentioned a few times—agricultural crop subsidies. The federal government spent $14.5 billion in direct payments to farmers in 2004.[4] That's about 1% of all income tax payments.

For the federal farm subsidy recipient, there's an even bigger incentive for the recipients to defend their program, because the distribution of benefits is severely lopsided.[5] In 2004, the most recent year for which comprehensive statistics are available, just 146,192 recipients received 62% of all the subsidies.[6] That's only 0.04% of the US population. Farm programs tend to favor a few well-connected companies, each of which has millions of dollars at stake as a result of receiving these generous subsidies. If there were ever an attempt to cut their subsidies, they would—and do—bring millions of dollars of lobbying power to bear on Congress.

Individual taxpayers, however, don't have the same sort of incentives to fight back. If taxpayers wanted to band together and pool their resources to lobby for a cut in farm subsidies, success would require a very large group of taxpayers. Lobbying doesn't come cheap, of course, and a group of taxpayers large enough to pay the lobbying bills would be hard to cobble together. No taxpayer has an incentive to contribute more than a few pennies on each tax dollar they pay to a lobbying effort against a specific government program. That's because even if the gang of taxpayers is successful in getting these government programs pared down, each member of the taxpayer coalition would only get a few pennies back. Thus, there is little coordinated taxpayer outcry, and the government programs survive.

Economist Mancur Olson explained this process forty years ago.[7] Olson pointed out that the disparity in incentives between taxpayers and what we now call "special interests" results from an inherent disadvantage of the larger group (i.e., taxpayers) compared to the smaller group (i.e., recipients of government dollars) in its ability to organize to defend its interests. It is this inherent bias in favor of the small special interest groups that provides a very robust explanation of why we still have Big Government, even though many taxpayers would prefer smaller government. "It would be in the best interest of those groups who are organizing to increase their own gains by whatever means possible," writes Olson. "This would include choosing policies that, though inefficient for the society as a whole, were advantageous for the

organized groups because the costs of the policies fell dispropor-
tionately on the unorganized."[8]

The divergence in who bears the costs of government programs in relation to who reaps the benefits serves as a built-in
structural defense of Big Government. In fact, many bureaucrats,
when their budgets are threatened, tell Congress that their
agency accounts for only a small share of the cost of government
borne by each citizen. Surely citizens wouldn't complain about
such a small expenditure, would they?

That was exactly the defense NEA chairwoman Jane
Alexander put forward in 1995 when the new Republican congressional majority attempted to eliminate funding for the arts.
"I do not believe," she said, "that the taxpayers . . . begrudge the
64 cents each year that the [NEA] costs them."[9] Mrs. Alexander's
math isn't exactly right. She simply divided the NEA budget by
the number of US citizens. Since there are fewer taxpayers
than citizens, the amount it costs each taxpaying citizen would
be a bit higher. But even if the estimate of 64 cents is a bit low,
the logic still holds. The proliferation of programs that make
up the modern-day federal government allows every bureaucrat to make this argument when an agency is under the budget
knife.

Or consider the fact that every time a government program is
created, an automatic constituency for its continued existence is
also created. All of the people the agency employs and all the ben-
eficiaries of the programs it administers have a greater incentive
and means to fight any threats to the program's existence than taxpayers do. Proposing to cut a program will be met with powerful
opposition. Bureaucrats operate as the political equivalent of a

street gang protecting their turf. Big Government begets more Big Government.

So if the arithmetic tends to favor Big Government, so does the institutional environment of Congress, which is dominated by special interests calling for more government spending. Take, for instance, congressional hearings. The list of witnesses is usually stacked with pro-spending voices. Payne analyzed the witness lists of major committee hearings between 1978 and 1986 and found that 95% of witnesses were supporters of more spending. Only 7% of the witnesses advocated cutting spending or were opponents of the programs. More than half of the witnesses (55%) were employed by government as either a federal bureaucrat, a state and local official, or a member of Congress.[10]

A study done in 1995 found that witnesses favoring more government spending outnumbered their opponents by a ratio of four to one. Thirty-five percent of witnesses were federal employees, and one of every three was a government grant recipient.[11] What's most remarkable is that the subject of this study was the first two years of the Republican Revolution, 1995 and 1996. Even though this was an improvement over the average from years past, it still shows how the message a congressman receives about federal spending is severely skewed, even in a year when Republicans were actively seeking to change the culture of Washington. The ratio has only gotten worse since then. Today there are many congressional committees that never hear from *any* voices pleading for lower spending during the course of an entire series of hearings.[12]

THE CURSE

Big Government by its very nature places federal politicians in the unique position of being able to choose winners and losers within the social and economic marketplace. Those lucky enough to be deemed winners would get plenty of special benefits at the expense of everybody else. It's a very seductive form of power, and it's hard to resist. And the longer a politician stays in office, the more a part of the system he becomes.

Call it the curse of incumbency.

The effects of the curse can be measured in dollar terms. The longer the Republicans remain the majority party in Congress, the longer their yearly spending wish lists become. This can be tracked in the annual data published by the National Taxpayers Union (NTU). They compile a list of all of the bills introduced or voted upon in each Congress and measure the overall impact of those bills. The bills to increase spending are placed alongside the bills to decrease spending. The result is what can be called the "net spending agenda" of members of Congress.

As you might expect, over time the culture of spending in Washington has chipped away at the fiscal discipline of Republicans. In the first Republican Congress (the 104th), the goal was to reduce government, so the net spending agenda of Republicans amounted to a spending cut of $18.5 billion in the House and a spending cut of $15.6 billion in the Senate. But in each subsequent Republican Congress, the bills to increase spending outstrip the bills to decrease spending. By the 108th Congress (2004–2005), the spending wish list for the House had grown to an increase of $35 billion and an increase of $34 billion in the Senate.[13]

You can measure how the Republican Congress has gone native in other ways, too. Each year, the NTU also scores members of Congress on how "fiscally conservative" they are in general—in other words, how disciplined they are at controlling spending and cutting taxes. A higher score tends to mean the member is more fiscally conservative. There has been a drop in the scores for Republicans in Congress as a whole over the past ten years. In 1995, the average score for a Republican in the House was around 83%, and in the Senate it was 86%. Today, the average score is 62% in the House and 71% in the Senate.

This is a trend also evident in the scores of the House members elected in 1994 who are still in office today. In 1995, their average score was 83%. Today, the average score is 61%. The score of some members dropped by only a few points, and others dropped by thirty points or more. But on the whole, the Class of 1994 acts much less conservatively on fiscal policy than they did in the 104th Congress.

Another symptom of the curse of incumbency is that members of Congress buy into the hype about what it takes to keep their power. One of the beliefs that many Republicans now hold is that in order to maintain the House and Senate majorities, they have to increase government spending. Yet many studies don't find much correlation between electoral outcomes and a politician's support for pork projects or bigger government. Payne conducted an analysis of reelection outcomes of the 1986 election and found that voting in favor of more spending had no positive effect on a congressman's margin of victory.[14]

Other scholars who have performed statistical analysis on election data on numerous elections between 1986 and 1994 found that—after adjusting for the sorts of things that would influence electoral outcomes, such as the advantage of being an incumbent, and macroeconomic conditions—voting in favor of spending cuts or against pork projects doesn't tend to hurt congressmen when they run for reelection. Or, to put it another way, there is no real significant advantage to supporting more government spending. Some studies even show that taking a stand against high spending might actually help a candidate.[15] That seems to fit with what we saw in the 1996 congressional election. Many budget-cutters were able to increase their vote share, despite a multimillion dollar campaign by the labor unions to unseat them, and a media echo chamber committed to the conventional wisdom that cutting the budget is bad politics.

Some members of Congress have been able to avoid the curse of incumbency. They were the ones who tended to view being in Congress as a temporary assignment, not a career. Members like Tom Coburn of Oklahoma and Mark Sanford of South Carolina pledged to serve only three terms in the House and then leave. They honored their pledge and were able to resist the lure of Washington's culture of spending. Indeed, many of these "self-limiters" were the main reason the Republican Revolution was able to accomplish anything at all.

Looking at the net spending agendas of these self-limiting members during the six years they served in the House, you find that they sponsored bills to cut spending on net every year they were in office. By the 106th Congress (1999-2000), their overall wish list was to cut the budget by $27.2 billion, while the overall

House Republican spending agenda was to increase it by $4.6 billion.[16] As Tom Coburn said of the self-limiters in the House, "Washington doesn't have anything we want. That's what makes us dangerous."[17] Today, Tom Coburn is in the Senate fighting vigorously for budget cuts, as we'll see in the concluding chapter. And his formula is still the same: Limit the number of terms you plan to serve—Coburn only wants to serve two in the Senate—and fight like hell for limited government the entire time.

There are current members of Congress who have not term-limited themselves, such as Jeff Flake of Arizona and Mike Pence of Indiana, who are able to resist the will to spend by simply being deeply committed to limited government. They pride themselves on eschewing the rituals of Washington and prefer to be back at home in their districts. But they are the exceptions to the rule.

There's a story, possibly apocryphal, about Reagan's days as governor of California. He was purported to have told his staff that if they ever used the word "we" not to refer to the people of California but instead to refer to the government of California, then it was time to leave Sacramento.[18] Frankly, it's hard to deny that being the incumbent party for so long has warped the thinking of Republicans in Washington. The culture of spending has changed their view of the world. After ten years in control of Congress and five in control of the White House, the cesspool the Republicans came to drain has started to feel more like a hot tub. They think of themselves as a permanent majority now. And the best friend of a permanent majority is Big Government.

IN DEFENSE
OF GRIDLOCK

*Why United Republican Government
Is a Bad Thing*

G ridlock is a friend of limited government.

To see what I mean, take a look at the table on this page. It shows the average yearly growth of government spending by president. It's also adjusted for inflation and measured in per capita terms. See if you can discern a pattern.

GROWTH OF GOVERNMENT BY PRESIDENT
(annualized real per capita growth)

Johnson	4.6%
Nixon/Ford	1.9%
Carter	2.9%
Reagan	1.7%
G.H.W. Bush	0.6%
Clinton	0.3%
G.W. Bush*	3.1%

*Through first five years

Here's a hint: Think about who controlled Congress during most of each of these presidencies. Presidents Johnson, Carter, and George W. Bush had a friendly House and Senate—meaning their respective political parties controlled both houses of Congress during most of their tenure. Political scientists call that united government. The rest of the presidents faced a Congress that was either completely or partly controlled by the opposition party. That's called *divided government.*

Now take a look at the table again in light of that. Notice that the presidents during a time of united government tended to preside over larger annual increases in government spending—around 3% or more—than those in times of divided government.

Economist William Niskanen has done some analysis of this phenomenon and found that it is not a fluke. Using a larger set of data that stretches back to President Truman, he found that the only periods of sustained fiscal restraint in the post-World War II era were under divided government, particularly the presidencies of Eisenhower and Clinton. The measure of government growth he used was real per capita growth in federal expenditures just as I have used in the previous table. Niskanen found that the average yearly growth of real per capita government expenditures was 1% under divided government. But under united government, spending grew by 5% each year on average.[1]

What if you look at the data in terms of how fast government grew in relation to the economy as measured by gross domestic product? The results still favor divided government. The average yearly increase in government above and beyond GDP growth in years of divided government was 0.04%. That's basically a rounding error. In the years of the united government, however, the average growth of government was 1% above the GDP trend.[2]

Divided government tends to have a beneficial impact on economic growth, too. Economist Richard Vedder has analyzed the trend of the unemployment rate, inflation rate, and growth of the stock market between 1971 and 1997 and found that gridlock is good. "When looking at three measures of economic well-being during the gridlock and non-gridlock years, without exception, the record is superior in the years of gridlock. The median unemployment rate was almost 15% lower in the years of split control than in the years when one party (in this case, the Democrats) had complete control. The stock market in the typical year rose nearly three times faster than when power was united. Even inflation, nominally controlled by the supposedly independent Federal Reserve System, was lower in a typical gridlock year."[3]

A more precise calculation of government growth would average the rates of growth in the budget on a year-by-year basis instead of grouping them together by presidential administration as in the previous table. That way we can account for those few years in the Reagan presidency (1987 and 1988) and the George W. Bush administration (part of 2001 and 2002) when the Senate was controlled by the Democrats. It also gives us the opportunity to see if any particular combination of divided government tends to yield less government growth. As you can see in the next table, the story doesn't change after analyzing the data in this way, either. On average, we are still better off under divided government.

UNITED VS. DIVIDED GOVERNMENT (1965–2006)
(average annual change in real per capita expenditures)

United Government (average)	3.4%
Democratic President and Democratic Congress	3.3%
GOP President and GOP Congress	3.6%
Divided Government (average)	1.5%
Democratic President and GOP Congress	0.4%
GOP President and Democratic House/GOP Senate	1.5%
GOP President and Democratic Congress	1.6%
GOP President and GOP House/Democratic Senate	4.3%

United government tends to lead to a 3.4% average annual increase in federal spending in real per capita terms—over double the growth under divided government. In fact, the only post-war years in which we've had a Republican president and a Republican Congress—the George W. Bush years—have tended to see faster budget growth than those in which we had united Democratic governments under Lyndon Johnson and Jimmy Carter. Yet none of these united government scenarios on average produced slower growth than most of the divided government scenarios.

In the divided government category, it seems the combination that delivered the slowest growth in government is that of a Democratic president and a GOP Congress. So, by this standard, the Clinton years of 1995 through 2000 should be preferable to fiscal conservatives than the current Bush administration. And by a wide margin, too. In those years, government was practically frozen in real per capita terms.

Next comes the combination of a Republican president and a GOP Senate, coupled with a Democratic House. This is what we saw during most of Reagan's presidency. A GOP president and a Democratic Congress—what we had under Nixon, Ford, and G.H.W. Bush—was the third best sort of outcome overall but only by a very small margin. Each of these divided government scenarios tended to be a good check on government growth on average.

The combination of a Republican president with a Democratic Senate and a GOP House has only occurred once over the past forty years—between the middle of 2001 and 2002, after Senator Jim Jeffords of Vermont left the Republican Party and handed control of the Senate to the Democrats. There is only two years of data for this combination, so there is not enough data to tell if it is less preferable to the others. So, there shouldn't be too much weight placed on this combination.

Why might divided government be more conducive to restrained spending? Increased defense spending under the united governments accounts for some of it. Niskanen noted in his analysis that defense spending varies widely over these years. Yet the correlation between wars and united governments is quite consistent. He points out that surveying US history uncovers a nearly 200-year-old pattern in which American participation in every war involving more than a few days of ground combat was initiated by a united government.

You could argue that this is mere coincidence. Or you could argue that united government creates an environment where there is less resistance from Congress when a president wants to exercise his powers as commander-in-chief. The burden of proof, however, is on those who suggest this is simply happenstance.

What is undeniable is that, even in a wartime scenario, a president and Congress have two choices of how to spend tax-payer money. This is the guns and butter trade-off discussed previously. In the periods of divided government, there is likely to be more pressure to offset new spending in one budget category with spending cuts in the other. In the periods of united government, however, that sort of pressure disappears. Instead, united government spawns large increases in across-the-board spending. That's exactly what we saw during the presidencies of Johnson, Carter, and now George W. Bush.

This is probably the best description of what we see under

united government, especially once you consider the nature of Washington politics. The one thing you can usually count on is partisanship. When Republicans are the beleaguered minority—or a congressional majority fighting a big-spending White House—they are in their element. Big Government is the clear enemy. But once they find themselves in control of it, they are less willing to throw a punch for fear they might hit their own teammates. After the GOP won control of both ends of Pennsylvania Avenue, as Jonathan Rauch wrote in the *Atlantic Monthly*, their approach changed. "Congressional Republicans and the White House egged each other on instead of reining each other in."[4]

We can see this by comparing how a GOP Congress treated the proposed nondefense budgets of Bill Clinton and George W. Bush. Remember that once the president's budget reaches Capitol Hill every year, Congress either increases or cuts the spending request. During the years of divided government under Clinton, a sort of gridlock effect ensued. The Republican Congress was happy to cut Clinton's domestic spending requests by an average of $9 billion each year between 1996 to 2001.

Contrast that with the budget outcomes under President Bush—specifically years in which, for the most part, there was an absence of gridlock. Between years 2003 and 2006, Congress passed, and Bush refused to veto, nondefense budgets that were an average of $16 billion *more* than the president proposed each year.

The rules of partisanship imply that a Big Government scheme proposed by a Republican president is more likely to be accepted by a Republican Congress than if it were proposed by a Democrat. That's exactly what happened with the Medicare drug benefit. It's quite likely the drug benefit would never have passed if it were proposed by, say, President Al Gore or President Hillary Clinton. And if the Medicare expansion did get traction in Congress, then Republican leaders would probably have been more interested in slowing it down and tacking on real reforms instead of abandoning the reform elements in the hope of speeding its passage as they did in 2003.

United government during the George W. Bush years has brought us the biggest expansion of government since Lyndon Johnson's Great Society—itself a product of united government under Democrats. Now consider what divided government has gotten us over the past 20 years. It gave us the 1986 tax reform, which chucked many of the complexities in the tax code and created a simpler and flatter tax system—indeed it was the closest we've ever come to a flat income tax. It gave us the Defense Base Closure and Realignment Act of 1990, which continues to save billions of dollars in the Pentagon budget. And it gave us the landmark welfare reform in 1996. In fact, all of these are examples of some of the grandest achievements of the limited-government movement.

It is possible that the sorts of Social Security reforms that supporters of limited government prefer would have a better chance of being enacted in a divided government, too. Those reforms could have been a reality in the Clinton years, for instance. In 1998, Clinton was on the verge of endorsing a plan to allow workers to divert a portion of their payroll taxes to invest in personal retirement accounts, just as President Bush has proposed. Then, the Republicans proceeded with their impeachment hearings, and that caused Clinton to abandon a plan that was likely to alienate Democrats at a time when he most needed their support.[5]

Some might argue that the pro-spending tendencies of the Republican Party today might be just as easily overcome by simply electing Republicans who are more deeply committed to limited government. But in order to vote for those sorts of people, they have to run for office in the first place. If the history of the modern Republican Party has shown us anything, it's that the chances of finding a candidate on the ballot who is genuinely committed to fighting for a smaller government is much higher in the wake of the GOP's overall rediscovery of the virtues of limited government. And that usually occurs only after Republicans have spent some time out of power as a result of losing a major election or two.

Reagan's success would not have been possible without Goldwater's landslide loss or, for that matter, Reagan's failed nomination run in 1976. The Republican Revolution was made possible only by George H.W. Bush's electoral trouncing. The candidates that Gingrich recruited were motivated not just by their outrage over the actions of the newly-elected Democratic president. They were also deeply compelled by a desire to return the party to its Reaganesque roots after Bush's betrayal on taxes. Contrast that with today where, after ten years in the majority, it looks like the GOP freshmen elected to Congress aren't motivated by the small government agenda of their predecessors. As the National Taxpayers Union reported in early 2006, the House Republican freshmen of the past two congresses have sponsored bills to increase spending faster than their senior House counterparts—a marked reversal of the trend seen in earlier Republican congresses.[6]

Divided government is the norm, not the exception, in

American politics since the 1950s. Since 1964 for instance, there were only thirteen years when we had united control of the legislative and executive branches of government at the federal level. The presidencies of Johnson and Carter account for nine of them. The past four years under George W. Bush account for the rest. What we've seen the past few years—a consolidated Republican majority—may simply be an anomaly.

If it does turn out to be an anomaly, is that such a bad thing for the supporters of limited-government? Based on the evidence here, it's probably not. In light of all this, fiscal conservatives need to ask themselves an important question: Even if you don't agree that a divided government would make us better off, can you really argue—based on the evidence here—that it would make us worse off?

THE BATTLE OF
NEW ORLEANS

The Fight for the Future of the GOP

Although nobody could have predicted it at the time, the next stage in the battle for heart and soul of the Republican Party has its roots in the events of 29 August 2005. That's the day Hurricane Katrina made landfall along the Gulf Coast, wiped out New Orleans, and tore through Mississippi and Alabama.

In the wake of the storm, Bush promised a domestic rebuilding effort for the Gulf Coast the likes of which had never been seen before. It would be a radical departure from previous federal relief efforts. Traditionally, the federal government would help clear debris, provide search-and-rescue assistance to states, hand out aid for displaced residents in the form of temporary housing assistance and unemployment benefits, and rebuild infrastructure the federal government had purview over, such as roads and bridges. The rest is left up to the states and the private sector.

Instead, a massive and permanent expansion of the federal role in response to this and future natural disasters, including long-term economic assistance, was what Bush had in mind. It was termed, by supporters and detractors alike, a Marshall Plan for the United States. He planned to give each displaced worker $5,000 of taxpayer money for job training. He proposed $2 billion in tax "incentives" to bring businesses back to the area. He wanted federal taxpayers to pick up the tab for the education expenses of all students forced to relocate, whether they attended private or public school.

Certainly the biggest part of the whole plan was the rebuilding of the Gulf Coast, but even that wasn't geared solely to fixing the infrastructure the federal government has control over, like bridges, levees, and roads. It was instead meant to be an open-ended commitment to rebuild the Gulf Coast, presumably everything from shopping malls to streetcars.[1] The original authors of the legislation decades ago that outlined the federal response after a natural disaster were worried about exactly this sort of open-ended assistance, and that's why they, according to the Congressional Research Service, did not "explicitly authorize the President to provide long-term recovery assistance to communities."[2]

Bush wasn't proposing that the federal government direct all of the rebuilding, but he was planning for it to pick up the tab. In what was basically the equivalent of handing state officials a blank check, Bush declared that the federal government was going to pay for "the great majority" of the cost of the rebuilding effort. Nor was the president doing much to try to keep state and local officials from going overboard in their requests for money. Instead, Bush was encouraging them. He made sure to tell state officials in Mississippi, for instance, to "think bold" when they made their recovery plans.[3]

The president had requested over $62 billion for the recovery effort by mid-September 2005. That amount dwarfed, in inflation-adjusted dollars, the $17.8 billion Congress spent on relief for victims of hurricanes Andrew, Iniki, and Omar in 1992, and the $15.2 billion appropriated for relief after the California earthquake in Northridge in 1994.

Some estimates suggested that Bush's commitments could, over time, cost in excess of $200 billion.[4] But when asked by reporters how they were going to pay for it all, the White House was mute. This instantly worried the fiscal conservatives in the House and Senate. They were still irked about the outrageous highway bill that had passed just two months before and had been enthusiastically embraced by Bush after he'd threatened a veto of a less expensive version. Now this?

The conservatives knew they had to beat the drum of fiscal discipline even harder to get spending cuts to offset the costs of Bush's newest plan to expand government. Not all of the conservatives were necessarily averse to the federal government having a role in the rebuilding process. They just wanted to make sure that the government could afford it all. Besides, there was a precedent set when the GOP Congress found offsetting budget cuts for the emergency appropriations after the Northridge earthquakes and the Oklahoma City bombings. The message was consistent with what fiscal conservatives had been advocating for the past five years: Strip away unnecessary spending to make room for the important stuff.

There was virtually no interest in that in GOP leadership circles. Josh Bolten, Bush's budget director (before being appointed White House chief of staff in April 2006), told reporters it was not realistic to find offsetting cuts elsewhere in the budget.[5] Later, Senator Tom Coburn of Oklahoma asked Bolten if he planned to pursue even some small budget reductions, and Bolten said he didn't have time to worry about that.[6]

Even the president seemed eager to avoid the question of whether his plans were affordable. When asked how big the tab might be, Bush sounded like he was channeling Yogi Berra: "It's going to cost whatever it costs."[7]

It was obvious the leadership on this one wasn't going to come from the White House, although that wasn't much of a surprise to the conservatives at this point. It certainly wasn't going to come from the congressional leaders, either. When some House conservatives tried to amend the initial emergency bill to fund the relief effort by adding a requirement for Congress to offset the costs, the House leaders ruled the amendment out of order and used parliamentary sleight-of-hand to defeat it.[8]

The main opponent of the fiscal conservatives in the House was their former ally, House majority leader Tom DeLay. Having gone native years before, he was the engineer of the biggest legislative defeats for conservatives lately, particularly the Medicare drug bill. Earlier in 2005, DeLay fought vigorously against the budget hawks as they tried to make some changes to the budget process. The changes would have had the effect of making it easier for Congress to restrain government spending.[9] An attempt to finally change the culture of spending was a goal that was obviously close to the hearts of the revolutionaries of 1994. Now it was considered legislative poison.

In mid-September 2005, Tom DeLay finally exposed how far the GOP leaders would go to perpetuate the myth that they were still the party of small government. In a speech to a packed room of reporters, he suggested that the Republicans had done so well at cutting spending the previous five years that it was time to declare an "ongoing victory" over budgetary fat. When he was asked by a perplexed reporter if he really meant to say that the government was running at peak efficiency, DeLay said, "Yes, after eleven years of [a] Republican majority we've pared it down pretty good." Feeling perhaps a bit too cocky, DeLay also said, "My answer to those that want to offset the spending is sure, bring me the offsets, I'll be glad to do it. But nobody has been able to come up with any yet."[10]

The Republican Study Committee—representing the fiscal conservatives in the House—had come up with numerous lists of spending cuts in previous years and presented them to the House leaders, so DeLay's comment was disingenuous at best. It was, however, an indication of the House leadership's state of denial on budget matters. When faced with the reality of their profligacy, it seemed the leadership's response was the political equivalent of putting their fingers in their ears and humming loudly.

In a closed-door meeting a few days later between House leaders, the only sort of commitment the conservatives got from their superiors was a vague promise to make sure there would be strong accountability of the new money being spent.[11] But the budget hawks didn't want platitudes about making sure the money didn't go to waste, a responsibility that Congress was supposed to assume anyway. They wanted real budget cuts.

After being met with so many brick walls on both ends of Pennsylvania Avenue, there was only one choice left for the fiscal conservatives. It was time to go nuclear.

The core members of the Republican Study Committee—particularly Representatives Jeff Flake of Arizona, Jeb Hensarling of Texas, and Mike Pence of Indiana, head of the RSC—knew the most effective weapon they had was the bad press they could generate for the GOP leaders. Their secret weapon in creating a lasting suspicion of the Republican record on the budget would turn out to be a pork project buried deep inside the highway bill: a bridge in Alaska (cost: $231 million) that would connect the city of Ketchikan to tiny Gravina Island (population: 50 people). The nickname of the project among critics was "the Bridge to Nowhere." It would be nearly as long as the Golden Gate Bridge and as high as the Brooklyn Bridge. Even the Anchorage Chamber of Commerce, a group usually eager to support infra-structure projects, opposed it.[12]

The project was just one of almost 6,000—many of them of dubious value—which were in the recently enacted highway bill. Yet it was the perfect poster child for the sorts of projects that the Republicans in Congress had become addicted to. The press response was overwhelming. Soon, reporters were digging up more ridiculous projects on their own.

The groundswell of disgust among rank-and-file Republicans at the state level was immense. "I don't think there's ever been more pressure at the grass-roots level to reduce spending," said Senator Jim DeMint of South Carolina. "I don't think we've had the sense of urgency that we are seeing now. And I don't think any politician is going to be able to ignore that."[13]

At first, the House leadership dealt with the situation as an entrenched and arrogant congressional majority usually does: It excoriated the rebels. In a closed-door meeting that was described by columnist Robert Novak as an "inquisition," Mike Pence was dragged before a panel of GOP leaders and lambasted for his heresy. The harshest treatment of Pence came from Tom DeLay, himself a previous head of the Republican Study Committee. The verbal beating was so intense that when he was offered a chair at another meeting later that day, Pence—a former radio-talk show host with a sense of humor—said he would be more comfortable standing since the GOP leaders had just tanned his hide.[14]

This treatment didn't silence the conservatives. It made them fight harder. On 21 September 2005, the Republican Study Committee launched what they called "Operation Offset." The goal was to apply even more pressure to the GOP leaders by putting the lie to DeLay's comments that there was no fat left to cut in the budget. The list of spending cuts the RSC produced could have been authored by David Stockman or John Kasich. It included over 100 ideas to offset relief spending, including eliminating many of the programs that were on the chopping block in the Contract with America budget.[15] The cuts amounted to over $100 billion in one-year savings.

The list included a proposal to delay the start of the Medicare drug benefit, and some members of the RSC were even pushing for outright repeal of that legislation. The other big item in the list was to cut $25 billion simply by terminating all the earmarks in the bloated highway bill. The budget hawks in the Senate— John McCain of Arizona, Tom Coburn of Oklahoma, John Sununu of New Hampshire, John Ensign of Nevada, and Jim DeMint and Lindsey Graham of South Carolina—also endorsed many of the same proposals, particularly the Medicare and highway bill offsets.[16]

As expected, all of the suggestions were met with opposition by GOP leaders. Tom DeLay was particularly vocal about his dislike of the proposals. He called the postponement of the Medicare benefit a "non-starter."[17] He even defended his own $114 million in pork projects from the highway bill. "My earmarks are pretty important to building an economy in that region," said DeLay.[18]

Such was the standard defense of the highway bill that the leadership and every defender of the highway projects used all year, but it was built on a fallacy. Government spending, even on highways, won't actually create any new economic growth or private-sector jobs in the aggregate. To spend money on anything, the government has to first tax that money out of the economy or borrow it from the capital markets. While supporters of a government project will argue that it creates employment for some, they fail to mention that the taxes or debt—a form of future taxes—will inhibit employment of others.

Experts within the federal government understand this. A 1993 study from the Congressional Research Service notes that employment gains from increased transportation spending would likely be offset by losses in other parts of the economy due to the increased taxes or debt to finance the spending. The authors of a 1992 Congressional Budget Office study even went so far as to ask an important question: "If [these proposals really create jobs], why not just keep adding new programs until full employment is achieved?"

Republicans used to ridicule Democrats for just the sorts of statement that DeLay had made in defense of the highway bill. Now GOP leaders were perpetuating the same fallacy. Even Speaker Dennis Hastert turned up his nose at tinkering with the highway bill. "It is exactly the highway bill we need," he said.[19]

Operation Offset had the desired effect of angering other senior Republicans, too. When a reporter asked Representative Don Young of Alaska whether he would consider forgoing the

"Bridge to Nowhere" project to help pay for relief to Hurricane Katrina victims, he barked, "Kiss my ear!"[20]

Even the White House spokesmen were being peppered with questions about why nobody seemed to be supporting spending offsets. In an interview with the *Wall Street Journal*, Bush's budget chief Josh Bolten was pressed to admit that "we should [not] rule anything out." Then later in the interview, he nixed the idea of postponing the prescription-drug benefit or getting rid of unnecessary highway projects.[21]

Still, the pressure worked. By October 2005, the president was publicly stating that spending cuts were indeed needed to pay for at least a part of the Katrina expenses.[22] The White House's preferred vehicle for doing so was a bill that would reduce expenditures for entitlement programs like food stamps and health programs. This sort of bill is called a "reconciliation bill" because it makes changes in the program funding formulas to bring the costs in line with the budget caps—in other words, it reconciles two legislative objectives.

But this approach, while certainly worthwhile, was hardly a bold step on behalf of increased fiscal discipline. The reconciliation bill was already in the hopper for that year and was already on the agenda before Hurricane Katrina had even formed. Advocating the bill's passage merely recommitted the administration to doing what they said they were planning to do at the beginning of the year anyway.

In addition, it was only by the twisted logic of Washington budgeting that overall savings in the reconciliation bill could be called a "cut." What the final form of legislation would do is simply reduce the increase of entitlement spending from 5.6% each year over the next five years to no more than 5.4% each year over the same period.[23] Republicans used to ridicule the Democrats for calling a reduction in the rate of growth a "cut." Now a Republican president was arguing that simply agreeing not to spend more money in the future was akin to a budget cut.

Besides, the amount of these so-called savings were only going to equal about $38 billion over five years, barely $7.5 billion per year. That assumes, of course, Congress and the president kept the promise not to hike spending at a later date. The conservatives were right to be worried about that, too. The last time a reconciliation bill passed was in 1997, and just one year after that, Congress hiked spending for all sorts of programs, particularly agriculture subsidies, that were supposed to have been "cut" every year after 1997.

The RSC pressure was still on Speaker Dennis Hastert, and he eventually agreed to commit to a small across-the-board cut in government spending in addition to passing the reconciliation bill.[24] But the change of heart probably had little to do with a concern over the GOP's big-spending ways. It probably had more to do with Hastert fearing for his job.

What seemed to be the driver of the later concessions by the House leadership was Tom DeLay's indictment on 28 September on charges that he had conspired to skirt campaign fundraising laws with a Texas political action committee he founded.[25] To abide by a rule that any House leader who has been indicted must leave their leadership post, DeLay stepped aside, and Representative Roy Blunt of Missouri, the House majority whip and DeLay protégé, became the interim majority leader.

With DeLay's future in doubt, there was a sense that the discontent among the conservatives could easily erupt into a call to overthrow all the House leaders. "Our real leverage has come from the fear that DeLay will not have a post to come back to," said Jeff Flake to a *Washington Post* reporter. "They are deathly afraid of a leadership election in January."[26]

DeLay was clearly conscious of the threat, too. He intended to beat the criminal charges against him and return to his leadership post, but before then he had to stage an act of contrition in order to mend some badly broken fences. Roughly a week after his indictment, DeLay told a closed meeting of the House Republican Conference, "I failed you." And then with a nod to the fiscal conservatives, he said, "You guys filled a void in the leadership."[27]

Meanwhile, the fiscal conservatives in the Senate were fighting a battle to defund the Bridge to Nowhere. Tom Coburn, the sponsor of an amendment to do that, went to the floor of the Senate and argued that it was time for senators to sacrifice a few of their sacred pork projects to help fund the rebuilding effort in New Orleans.

Senator Ted Stevens of Alaska, on the other hand, disagreed vehemently and howled at Coburn. "This amendment is an offense to me," he yelled. After calming down only a bit, he reminded everyone that he was one of the most senior senators in the body and suggested that Coburn's audacious stand in favor of fiscal discipline was not welcome, especially since it was coming from a freshman senator. Stevens even threatened to resign if the amendment passed. Luckily for Stevens but unfortunately for taxpayers, the amendment was defeated by 82–15.[28]

The battle may have been lost, but the war wasn't over. The

Republicans, tired of all the bad press, eventually agreed a month later to eliminate the requirement that Alaska build the Bridge to Nowhere. However, the money was not redirected to the New Orleans rebuilding effort. It was still headed to Alaska, making the action of terminating the earmark merely symbolic.[29]

The fiscal conservatives were finally able to force the leadership into a 1% across-the-board spending cut and a larger reconciliation bill than would have existed otherwise. Yet even that bill couldn't pass without some sweeteners for the big spenders, including more agriculture subsidies for milk producers, and $1.4 billion over five years to help poor families buy digital television sets.[30] Even with the 1% across-the-board cut in spending, the federal government was going to grow over 6% in inflation-adjusted terms, the biggest increase in sixteen years. One shudders to think about how much bigger the budget might have been if the RSC hadn't gone nuclear.

A CHANGE IN COURSE?

By 2006, it was obvious that if the GOP were going to change its image, it would need a new majority leader. And not just any new leader, but one committed to controlling spending and reforming the budget process. Yet House Speaker Dennis Hastert had no intention of budging in his support for DeLay. So Jeff Flake of Arizona circulated a petition in the House to call for an immediate election. He announced he had at least half the signatures he needed on 7 January 2006.[31] That same day, DeLay yielded to the pressure and agreed to relinquish his claim to the leadership job.[32]

The election of the new House majority leader was perhaps the first real chance for the GOP to change course. The leading candidate for DeLay's job was interim majority leader, Roy Blunt of Missouri—a close associate of Tom DeLay. Blunt was called a "maestro of earmarks" by the press, and was one of the primary behind-the-scenes critics of the RSC for daring to embarrass the GOP by speaking the truth about the party's fiscal record.[33] John Boehner of Ohio was the candidate with one foot in the reform camp (he had never accepted an earmark in any legislation) and another in the lobbying realm (he kept a "K Street Cabinet" of loyal lobbyists who were waiting to help run the show if he won).[34] The congressman that conservatives saw as the true reform candidate—and, thus, the obvious dark horse in the race—was John Shadegg of Arizona, former leader of the RSC and the man who called the basement meeting in the Longworth House Office Building that was described in the opening chapter of this book.

The theme of their campaigns was the need for an aggressive reform agenda to change the relationship between Congress and K Street. Each candidate claimed they would be the most effective at changing the image of the GOP. Shadegg, knowing he was unlikely to win, eventually threw his support behind Boehner, who was seen by the conservatives as at least preferable to Blunt. That clinched the win for the congressman from Ohio when the election was held at the end of January 2006.

When it finally came time to start cleaning up how the Republicans did business, however, the new leadership team still wasn't quite willing to go as far as necessary to really change the culture of spending in Congress. The lobbying reforms the GOP pushed tended to focus more on restricting the amounts and types of gifts that lobbyists could award to congressmen, such as meals and luxurious trips. But even the lobbying community knew any sort of restriction like that could easily be evaded. Typical of the view on K Street was a comment by J. Steven Hart of Williams & Jensen, a major lobbying firm, reported in the *Washington Post.* "If meals are heavily restricted," he said, "we're likely to see executives from the home office picking up checks because they're not lobbyists."[35]

Other reforms, such as those preferred by senators like John McCain of Arizona, were aimed at the amount of money candidates can receive from lobbyists for their campaign. Yet that sort of restriction is also only likely to encourage lobbyists to find other more innovative ways to evade the caps or reward congressmen in a manner that the reformers could not possibly predict.

Besides, the increase in campaign spending that worries campaign reformers is not the driver of Big Government's growth. It's the other way around. Recall that special interests are always interested in winning more favors from politicians. As government gets bigger, so does the number of favors politicians are able to grant. And the money spent on obtaining those favors— including donations to political campaigns—also increases. As a study in the *Journal of Law and Economics* found, 87% of the rise in campaign spending is directly attributable to the growth in government.[36]

The reforms favored by many Republicans are aimed at treating the symptoms but not the disease. The disease is a federal government that allows politicians to tax everyone to deliver benefits to special interests. Take away the ability of Congress to deliver the goodies and you take away the incentive of lobbyists and political action committees to spend so much time and money to influence the contents of an appropriations bill. Thus, Republicans can only really solve the problem by loosening their embrace of Big Government altogether. That's what the current battle for the heart and soul of the Republican Party should be about.

FULL CIRCLE

On the morning of 8 April 1957, in the fifth year of Eisenhower's presidency, Senator Barry Goldwater of Arizona received a call from the White House. He was being invited by the president to chat about Goldwater's upcoming reelection campaign. But the senator declined the invitation. Instead, Goldwater had made a fateful decision that morning. He planned to denounce Eisenhower's new budget on the floor of the Senate that afternoon. At the time, it was the largest budget ever proposed in peacetime. The speech would prove to be one of the most important of Goldwater's career. It was his declaration of independence from the "me-too" Republicanism of the 1950s.

"Just as I campaigned against waste, extravagance, high taxes, unbalanced budgets, and deficit spending in the recent Democratic administrations, so shall I also, if necessary, wage a battle of conscience and conviction against the same elements of fiscal irresponsibility in this Republican administration," boomed Goldwater. "In America we have no double standard of governmental soundness. What is bad under the leadership of one party cannot possibly be good under the leadership of the other."

He accused the president of embracing "government by bribe" and warned of the decline of the GOP as a true defender of liberty. "It is equally disillusioning to see the Republican Party plunging headlong into the same dismal state experienced by the traditional Democrat principles of Jefferson and Jackson during the days of the New Deal and the Fair Deal. As a result of those economic and political misadventures, that once great party has now lost its soul of freedom; its spokesmen today are peddlers of the philosophy that the Constitution is outmoded, that states rights are void, and that the only hope for the future of these United States is for our people to be federally born, federally housed, federally clothed, federally educated, federally supported in their occupations, and to die a federal death, thereafter to be buried in a federal box in a federal cemetery."

He identified the culprit of the GOP's decline: "the strange and mysterious force" of creeping liberalism in the party. "When are we Republicans . . . going to learn that we can no longer win elections in this country by playing the role of a political Santa Claus?" asked Goldwater. "We may not, any of us, be here to witness the ultimate consequences of a continuation of this trend," he concluded. "But history would not forget that ours was the challenge forfeited."[37]

That same speech could be delivered tomorrow on the floor of the Senate or House, and every criticism would still ring true. The sad truth is that the GOP today has finally regressed into the sort of party that Barry Goldwater was fighting to change almost fifty years ago. A party that, nineteen months after Goldwater delivered his Senate floor speech, was slaughtered politically in the 1958 election. (It was one of the biggest losses in the party's history—the GOP lost forty-eight seats in the House and thirteen in the Senate that year.) A party that, instead of making a principled case for limited government, set the stage for united Democratic control of Congress and the White House that began with the election of John F. Kennedy, continued with Lyndon Johnson, and brought us an even larger expansion of government during the Great Society era.

George W. Bush and the Republican leaders in Congress have effectively put the GOP on the same path that Eisenhower chose in 1957. It's been enough to spur liberal GOP senator Arlen Specter of Pennsylvania to announce gleefully in March 2006, "The Republican Party is now principally moderate, if not liberal!" That might be a bit of wishful thinking on Specter's part. Yet the record of the GOP over the past five years implies that he is probably right. No, Republicans weren't the first to use the federal government as a favor factory. But they have proven that when it comes to expanding government, they are fast learners, eager participants, and savvy innovators.

The Republican Party is no longer one that stands athwart federal bloat yelling, "Stop!" Today it is one that stands beside the federal behemoth and cries, "Full steam ahead!" It is a party that seems more interested in providing late-night television huckster Matthew Lesko with more material for the next edition of his *Big Fat Book of Free Money for Everyone* than in fighting for limited government.

The GOP has come full circle. Say goodbye to the party of Reagan and Goldwater.

Welcome to the party of Matthew Lesko.

ACKNOWLEDGMENTS

To my knowledge, there isn't a support group for first time authors. But I really didn't need one. I was surrounded by wonderful people throughout the process of writing this book, and I was lucky enough to have their advice and encouragement to draw upon.

The Cato Institute provides unmatched freedom to its analysts to pursue research that some might find politically incorrect. Many thanks to Cato's founder and president, Ed Crane, for building such a great institution and granting me the honor of working there. Special thanks also go to David Boaz, Cato's executive vice president, who was especially supportive of my work on this book and provided invaluable comments on the manuscript.

Other colleagues at the Cato Institute were very helpful, too. The graphic design team of John Meyers and Kelly Anne Creazzo created the beautiful charts that appear in this book. Michael Cannon and Neal McCluskey provided excellent comments on the Medicare and education sections in this book. Tom Firey gave me suggestions in the formative stages of the manuscript. Tyson Schritter and Elliot Wolfe provided vital research assistance.

I've never actually met Mr. Alex Piek, but he is the father of a friend of mine (Gina) and a good conservative in the Reagan tradition. He was just the sort of person I had in mind as my main audience while writing this book. If he enjoys reading it, I'll consider myself successful.

My old friend and partner-in-crime, Dave Peterson, gave me the story about being a substitute teacher in Arizona that I used to open Chapter 2.

My dear friends P.J. and Erin Doland were a great source of diversion when I needed to take a break from writing this book. They were good at playing the role of occasional sounding board as well.

Jeremy Lott—fellow first-time author—got me an audience with the editors at Nelson Current. The book might not have existed without him.

Garrett Brown is a good friend and my sage guide through the bizarre world that is the publishing industry. My book proposal would not have been half as good without him, and he was always quick to provide direction and an encouraging word.

Huge thanks go to my editor, Joel Miller. He has an amazing ability to turn my words into something worth reading. And he's a great guy. Patient, too. In terms of editors, I think I'm spoiled.

My brother David has always been one of my biggest fans. I owe him a lifetime of thanks not just for being such a wonderful brother but also because he taught me how to look good on television.

My parents have been tremendously supportive of everything I've pursued in life. They know writing a book has always been a dream of mine. Part of that dream was dedicating my first book to them. So I have. They truly deserve it.

Finally, to my wife, Krystal. You make me the happiest man on the planet. You are endlessly supportive. You are my muse.

NOTES

CHAPTER 1—From the Cesspool to the Hot Tub

1. Quoted in Nancy E. Roman, "Republicans Retreat from Battle to Shrink the Size of Government," *Washington Times*, 4 March 1999, A1.
2. Janet Hook, "President Putting 'Big' Back into Government," *Los Angeles Times*, 8 February 2005, A1.
3. Quoted in Sheryl Gay Strolberg, "The Revolution That Wasn't," *New York Times*, 13 February 2005, W1.
4. George Washington University/Lake Snell Perry and Associates Battleground Poll, 28-31 March 2004, available at http://www.lspma.com/polls/pdf/9701Q.pdf; and George Washington University/Tarrance Battleground Poll, 12-15 February 2006, available at http://www.tarrance.com/battleground/030206/10420Q.pdf.
5. John Harwood, "Republican Edge on Key Issues Is Slipping amid Party's Setback,: Wall Street Journal, 10 November 2005, A1.
6. Karlyn Bowman, "Attitudes Toward the Federal Government," *American Enterprise Institute Studies in Public Opinion*, 6 August 2003.
7. Rasmussen Reports, 16 February 2004.
8. Ibid.
9. Darren K. Carlson, "Big Government, Big Threat?" Gallup News Service, 28 December 2004.

CHAPTER 2—Why Reagan Matters

1. The dramatic story of the 1976 campaign is told in vivid detail by Craig Shirley in *Reagan's Revolution* (Nelson Current, 2005).
2. William Greider, "The Education of David Stockman," *Atlantic Monthly*, December 1981.
3. William Niskanen, *Reaganomics: An Insider's Account of the Policies and the People* (Oxford University Press, 1988), 292.
4. Martin Anderson, *Revolution* (Harcourt Brace Jovanovich, 1988), 247.
5. David Stockman, *The Triumph of Politics* (Harper and Row, 1986), 101–102.
6. Quoted in David Frum, *Dead Right* (Basic Books, 1994), 42.
7. Ibid, 109.
8. Stockman, 110.
9. Bernard Weintraub, "National Coalition to Battle Reagan Budget Cutbacks," *New York Times*, 28 February 1981.
10. Bernard Weintraub, "Feminist Groups Attack Reagan Budget Cutbacks," *New York Times*, 27 March 1981.
11. Anderson, 243.
12. Stockman, 143.
13. Ibid.
14. Stockman, 154.
15. Martin Tolchin, "Senate Rejects Bid to Restore Welfare Funds," *New York Times*, 1 April 1981.
16. Stockman, 174.
17. Hendrick Smith, "Second Honeymoon," *New York Times*, 29 April 1981.
18. Steven Roberts, "Democrats in House Fear Reagan Budget Cannot Be Altered," *New York Times*, 28 April 1981.
19. Martin Tolchin, "It's Reagan's Strong Suit Against the Odds," *New York Times*, 3 May 1981.
20. This story is recounted in Stockman, 175–176.
21. Helen Dewar, "Reagan's Budget Plan Wins Easily in House," *Washington Post*, 8 May 1981, A1.
22. Stockman, 183.
23. Niskanen, 37.
24. Stockman, 191.

25. Stockman, 208.

26. Stockman, 221.

27. Stockman, 204, 228.

28. Niskanen, 63.

29. Robert G. Kaiser, "Probably Good Politics, but Budget Problems Remain Unsolved," *Washington Post*, 24 November 1981, A6.

30. Lee Lescaze, "Federal Shutdown Ends as Reagan, Hill Agree," *Washington Post*, 24 November 1981, A1.

31. Author's calculations based on numbers from the Office of Management and Budget cited in "Warriors Against Inflation," by Bruce Bartlett, *National Review*, 14 January 2004, available at: http://www.nationalreview.com/nrof_bartlett/bartlett 200406140846.asp.

32. Niskanen, 77.

33. See Paul Johnson, *A History of the American People* (Harper Collins, 1997), 929–931. Also see Paul Lettow, *Ronald Reagan and His Quest to Abolish Nuclear Weapons* (Random House, 2005); and John Lewis Gaddis, *The Cold War: A New History* (Penguin, 2006).

34. Niskanen, 29–30.

35. The number of terminated programs comes from Jonathan Rauch, *Government's End: Why Washington Stopped Working* (Public Affairs, 1999), 180.

CHAPTER 3—The Short-Lived Revolution

1. Lewis L. Gould, *Grand Old Party* (Random House, 2003), 447.

2. Author's calculations based on data from the Office of Management and Budget.

3. Bruce Bartlett, *Impostor: How George W. Bush Bankrupted America and Betrayed the Reagan Legacy* (Doubleday, 2006), 124.

4. For a description of the key events that led up to the Republican Revolution in 1994, see chapter 2 of Major Garrett, *The Enduring Revolution: How the Contract with America Continues to Shape the Nation* (Crown Forum, 2005).

5. Elizabeth Drew, *Showdown: The Struggle Between the Gingrich Congress and the Clinton White House* (Touchstone, 1996), 14.

6. John Harwood, "Revolution II: Reagan-Era Politicians Are Now

Determined to Revive '80s Policies," *Wall Street Journal Europe*, 4 January 1995, 1.

7. Ibid.
8. Drew, 126.
9. David Maraniss and Michael Weisskopf, *Tell Newt to Shut Up!* (Touchstone, 1996), 37.
10. Drew, 127.
11. Linda Killian, *The Freshmen* (Westview Press, 1998), 31.
12. Killian, 13.
13. Ibid.
14. Drew, 124.
15. Ibid., 125.
16. This story comes from Killian, 27.
17. Guy Gugliotta, "GOP House Freshmen Put Cabinet Posts on Block," *Washington Post*, 15 February 1995, A7.
18. Drew, 128.
19. The story of these concessions are told in chapter 4 of Maraniss and Weisskopf.
20. Janet Hook, "House OKs GOP Budget, Deep Cuts," *Los Angeles Times*, 19 May 1995, 3.
21. National Public Radio, "All Things Considered," 4 January 1995.
22. Drew, 240.
23. On the Senate's reluctance to balance the budget and eliminate more than 100 programs, see Drew, p. 208 and 242. On Clinton's budget plan, see Office of Management and Budget, *Budget of the US Government, Fiscal Year 1996* (GPO, 1995), 3.
24. David E. Rosenbaum, "Congress Passes GOP's Budget-Balancing Plan," *New York Times*, 30 June 1995, 1.
25. George Hager and Alissa J. Rubin, "Last-Minute Maneuvers Forge a Conference Agreement," *Congressional Quarterly*, 27 June 1995.
26. See "Congress Enacts GOP-led Budget," *St. Louis Post-Dispatch*, 30 June 1995.
27. Sharon Moloney, "Deficit Hawk Kasich Says GOP 'Saving the Country,'" *Cincinnati Post*, 26 June 1995.
28. Killian, 106–107.
29. Ibid., 107–108.

30. Ibid., 120–121.

31. Stephen Moore and Dean Stansel, "How Corporate Welfare Won: Clinton and Congress Retreat from Cutting Business Subsidies," *Cato Institute Policy Analysis No. 254*, 15 May 1996.

32. Moore and Stansel, 1.

33. Brian Kelly, "The Pork That Just Won't Slice," *Washington Post*, 10 December 1995, C1.

34. Dan Morgan, "Republicans on Key Panel Appropriate Policy Role," *Washington Post*, 22 July 1995, A8; and Killian, 120–122.

35. Author's calculations based on numbers from the *Budget of the US Government, Appendix*, various years.

36. Stephen Slivinski, "The Corporate Welfare Budget: Bigger Than Ever," *Cato Institute Policy Analysis No. 415*, 10 October 2001.

37. Dan Morgan and Eric Pianin, "Doing the Dirty Work of Deficit Reduction," *Washington Post*, 9 July 1995, A1.

38. Drew, 259.

39. Mary Agnes Carey, "Gingrich, Armey Promise to Kill Commerce Dept. In Fall," Dow Jones News Service, 27 July 1995.

40. Morgan and Pianin, 9 July 1995.

41. Karen Tumulty, "Your Knife or Mine?" *Time*, 26 June 1995, 34.

42. David Rogers, "As Clinton Is Set to Sign Spending Bill, House GOP Plans Second Wave of Cuts," *Wall Street Journal*, 24 July 1995, A2.

43. Karen Tumulty, 26 June 1995.

44. Roger K. Lowe, "Kasich to Be Fiscal 'Enforcer,'" *Columbus Dispatch*, 1 July 1995, A1.

45. Maraniss and Weisskopf, 99–109; and Killian, 148-151.

46. Lowe, 1 July 1995.

47. Killian, p. 110–112.

48. Davis, 258.

49. Rene Sanchez, "House GOP Issues Plans for Eliminating Departments," *Washington Post*, 24 May 1995, A23.

50. Author's calculations based on press release from the House Appropriations Committee, "Appropriations Panel Fulfills Commitment to Cut Government," December 1995.

51. Dan Morgan, "GOP: Spending Bill Sends Clear Signals on Priorities; Democrats Decry Work of 'Wrecking Crew,'" *Washington Post*, 5 August 1995, A1.

52. Drew, 336.

53. Tom Coburn, *Breach of Trust* (Nelson Current, 2003), 59–61.

54. Drew, 372.

55. John Yang, "Indiana Pair Feel the Wrath of Gingrich; Speaker to Skip Fund-Raising Events after Freshmen's Votes on Shutdown," *Washington Post*, 11 January 1996, A6.

56. Jerry Gray, "Both Congress and Clinton Find Cause for Cheer in the Final Budget Deal," *New York Times*, 26 April 1996, 22.

57. Garrett, 128.

58. Killian, 405–413.

59. Ibid., 160–161.

60. Daniel J. Palazzolo, *Done Deal: The Politics of the 1997 Budget Deal* (Chatham House, 1999), 184–185.

61. For a detailed discussion of the 1996 welfare reforms and its success, see Michael Tanner, *The Poverty of Welfare: Helping Others in Civil Society* (Cato Institute, 2003).

62. For a detailed discussion of how pre-1996 farm programs operated and how the 1996 reforms changed the programs for the better, see Chris Edwards and Tad DeHaven, "Farm Subsidies at Record Levels as Congress Considers New Farm Bill," *Cato Institute Briefing Paper No. 70*, 18 October 2001.

63. Author's calculations based on data from the Office of Management and Budget.

CHAPTER 4—The Smell of Marble

1. This story is related by Representative Van Hilleary of Tennessee to author Linda Killian, *The Freshmen* (Westview Press, 1998), 419.

2. See Paul Craig Roberts, "Newt Should Keep His Eye on the Enemy: Big Government," *Business Week*, 13 January 1997, 26; and David Rogers, "Gingrich Narrowly Retains Speaker Position in Vote that Severely Weakens His Power," *Wall Street Journal*, 8 January 1997, A24.

3. Paul Gigot, "Newt or Not, Does Anyone Have an Agenda?" *Wall Street Journal*, 10 January 1997, A10.

4. Jerry Gray, "Gingrich Offers an Agenda, but the Christian Coalition Attacks Sharply," *New York Times*, 7 March 1997, 20.

5. Katharine Q. Seelye, "Former Allies Torment Gingrich," *New York Times*, 9 March 1997, 1.

6. Guy Gugliotta, "House Dissenters Block Campaign Probe Funds; Vote Described as Rebuke of GOP Leadership," *Washington Post*, 21 March 1997, A1.

7. Ibid.

8. This story is synopsized from the account in Tom Coburn, *Breach of Trust* (Nelson Current, 2003), 72–80.

9. Jerry Gray, "Conservative Senators Pressure GOP Leaders in Budget Talks," *New York Times*, 23 April 1997, 1.

10. David E. Rosenbaum, "Gingrich on a Slippery Surface with a Firm Base," *New York Times*, 25 March 1997, 22.

11. Robert Novak, "GOP Surrenders with Budget Pact," *Chicago Sun-Times*, 5 May 1997, 25.

12. Patrice Hill, "Budget Accord Clears Senate on 78–22 Vote; Lott Calls It Best Deal in Decades," *Washington Times*, 24 May 1997, A1.

13. Gerald F. Seib and John Harwood, "Right and Left Will Likely Accept Deal, but Not with a Whole Lot of Enthusiasm," *Wall Street Journal*, 29 July 2001, A2.

14. Coburn, 92–93.

15. Donald Lambro, "GOP Conservatives Slap Budget Plan as Bad Deal for Party," *Washington Times*, 25 May 1997, A4.

16. Robert Novak, "GOP Rank and File Up in Arms," *Chicago Sun-Times*, 11 May 1997, 35.

17. Greg Hitt, "Budget Pact Hurts Some GOP Lawmakers Down Home," *Wall Street Journal*, 5 January 1998, A24.

18. Ibid.

19. Newt Gingrich, *Lessons Learned the Hard Way* (Harper Collins, 1998), 22–24.

20. Robert Novak, "Pork Still No. 1 on House Menu," *Chicago Sun-Times*, 2 April 1998, 37.

21. Eric Pianin, "Clinton, Congress Finding Ways to Juggle Spending Limits," *Washington Post*, 22 March 1998.

22. Ibid.

23. Coburn, 94.

24. Ibid., 100.

25. Novak, 2 April 1998.

26. Jim Myers, "Largent: Vote Not for Sale," *Tulsa World*, 20 March 1998, 1.

27. Jim Myers, "Largent, Coburn Spurn Millions, Both Decry 'Dirty Politics,' Say Special Road Projects Effort to Buy Votes," *Tulsa World*, 25 March 1998, 1.

28. Novak, 2 April 1998.

29. Coburn, 106–107.

30. Gabriel Roth, "Liberating the Roads: Reforming US Highway Policy," *Cato Institute Policy Analysis No. 538*, 17 March 2005, 12–13.

31. These examples come from research by Citizens Against Government Waste, cited in Coburn, 95–96; and Joe Scarborough, *Rome Wasn't Burnt in a Day* (Harper, 2004), 110.

32. Eric Pianin, "Representative Kasich Stirs up a Low-Calorie Budget; Chairman Wants to Lose an Additional $154 Billion and Shuck Two Departments," *Washington Post*, 26 April 1998, A4.

33. Christopher George, "Surplus Could Hit $60 Billion This Year–Late April's Tax Payments, Bigger Than Expected, Drive Forecasts Higher," *Wall Street Journal*, 5 May 1998, A2.

34. Robert Novak, "GOP Agenda Is Withering Away," *Chicago Sun-Times*, 11 May 1998, 31.

35. Mark L. Melcher and Stephen R. Soukup, "Potomac Perspective," *Prudential Securities Investor Weekly*, 21 October 1998, 41.

36. See Citizens Against Government Waste, "CAGW Blasts Omnibus Spending Bill as a National Disgrace," Press release, 20 October 1998; "Losing the Revolution," *National Review*, 9 November 1998; and Ralph Bennet and Daniel Levine, "The Great 1999 Budget Rip-Off," *Reader's Digest*, February 1999, 99–102.

37. David Rogers, "Budget Pact Reverses '97 Fiscal Discipline of the GOP," *Wall Street Journal*, 16 October 1998, A16.

38. Congressional Budget Office, "Emergency Spending under the Budget Enforcement Act: An Update," 8 June 1999.

39. Daniel Griswold, Stephen Slivinski, and Chris Preble, "Ripe for Reform: Six Good Reasons to Reduce US Farm Subsidies and Trade Barriers," *Cato Institute Trade Policy Analysis No. 30*, 14 September 2005.

40. Charles Babcock, "'Emergency' Funding Creates Windfall of Bonus Bucks," *Washington Post*, 4 November 1998, A4.

41. For evidence on class size having no effect on educational achievement, see Eric Hanushek, "The Evidence on Class Size," *University of Rochester Occasional Paper 98-1*, February 1998, available at http://www.wallis.rochester.edu/WallisPapers/wallis_10.pdf. Republicans who followed education policy were aware of the study at the time and could have easily made a case that Clinton's proposal would not make a difference and would simply waste money in the process.

42. Major Garrett, *The Enduring Revolution* (Crown Forum, 2005), 160–161.

43. Ralph Bennet and Daniel Levine, *Reader's Digest*, February 1999.

44. Coburn, 124–125.

45. Babcock, *Washington Post*, 4 November 1998.

46. Coburn, 131.

47. Katherine Seelye, "Gingrich Draws Fire from the Right," *New York Times*, 25 October 1998, 24.

48. Guy Gugliotta, "Some in GOP Appalled, Many Democrats Pleased with Budget Deal," *Washington Post*, 16 October 1998, A17.

49. George F. Will, "Republicans as Red Sox," *Newsweek*, 26 October 1998.

50. Seelye, 25 October 1998.

51. Garrett, 160.

52. Data on congressional elections can be found at the website of the Office of the Clerk, US House of Representatives, http://clerk.house.gov/members/electionInfo/elections.html.

53. Greg Hitt, "GOP's Hastert Looks at Easing Spending Limits," *Wall Street Journal*, 25 February 1999, A2.

54. John M. Broder, "Clinton Offers His Budget, and the Battle Begins," *New York Times*, 2 February 1999, 1.

55. Richard W. Stevenson, "Congress on Path to Approve a Rise in Spending Caps," *New York Times*, 28 February 1999, 1.

56. Richard W. Stevenson, "Support is Pledged for Republican Budget," *New York Times*, 10 March 1999, 14.

57. Helen Dewar and Juliet Eilperin, "GOP Fears Agenda Drift as 2000 Elections Near," *Washington Post*, 24 May 1999, A3.

58. Coburn, 147–162.

59. Eric Pianin and George Hager, "Congress Making Greater Use of Creative Accounting," *Washington Post*, 16 October 1999, A15.

60. Eric Pianin, "GOP Seeks to Ease Crunch with 13-Month Fiscal Year," *Washington Post*, 14 September 1999, A1.

61. Ibid.

62. Eric Pianin, "In Session: Congress; Climate Is Cooler for Kasich's Budget Scolding," *Washington Post*, 11 October 1999, A23.

63. David Bauman and Richard E. Cohen, "A Budget Deal with Political Cover for All," *National Journal*, 20 November 1999, 340.

64. Author's calculations based on data from the Office of Management and Budget and House Report 105–116, 14 June 1997.

65. Helen Dewar, "Smidgen of Growth in $1.8 Trillion Plan; GOP Budget Blueprint Would Grow Defense, Provide for Tax Cuts," *Washington Post*, 11 March 2000, A10.

CHAPTER 5—Selling Out

1. David Bauman, "Finding It Hard to Say, 'No,'" *National Journal*, 13 July 2002.

2. Michael Weisskopf, "The Penny Pincher in Chief," *Time*, 8 January 2001, 27.

3. Jacob Schlesinger, "The Enforcer: Bush Budget Director Jousts with Congress, and Big Fight Is Likely," *Wall Street Journal*, 15 August 2001, A1.

4. Lee Walczak and Richard S. Dunham, "The Man Who Would Be Reagan," *Business Week*, 29 January 2001, 32.

5. Weisskopf, 8 January 2001.

6. Glenn Kessler, "OMB Chief Looks to Slow Budget's Growth," *Washington Post*, 2 February 2001, A5.

7. Congressional Budget Office, "The Budget and Economic Outlook: Fiscal Years 2002–2011," January 2001.

8. Mike Allen and Glenn Kessler, "Bush Sends Tax Cut Plan and Economic Warning," *Washington Post*, 9 February 2001, A1.

9. Mike Allen, "Bush Touts Tax Plan as Congress Awaits Proposal," *Washington Post*, 7 February 2001, A4.

10. Author's analysis based on data from the Office of Management and Budget, *Budget of the United States Government, Fiscal Year 2002* (Government Printing Office, 2001); also, Stephen Slivinski, "The Corporate Welfare Budget: Bigger Than Ever," *Cato Institute Policy Analysis No. 415*, 10 October 2001, 7–8.

11. Author's analysis based on data from the Office of Management and Budget, *Budget of the United States Government, Fiscal Year 2002*, 7–8.

12. Author's calculations based on ibid. A note about budget calculations is worth mentioning here. The federal budget includes two numbers for every government spending program: Budget authority and outlays. Budget authority is the amount that Congress and the president allow an agency to commit to spending in the current fiscal year or a future one. Outlays are the amount that an agency actually spends in the current year. When making budget comparisons, budget analysts tend to focus on outlays since that is the amount of money that the government actually spends in a year. Budget authority numbers, by nature, are often lower than outlays and can be manipulated to move spending into future years. Supporters of the White House tend to only look at budget authority data, but that yields an inaccurate picture of how much the government is actually spending. In fact, the use of budget authority numbers allows them to allege that spending is growing slower under Bush when it actually isn't. Those same defenders of the White House often claim that counting outlays tars Bush with budget increases that actually started under Clinton. This is bogus. If Bush and Republicans in Congress wanted to stop that money from being spent, they could have. Therefore, all

the budget figures cited in this book, unless otherwise noted, are outlays.

13. Office of Management and Budget, Budget of the United States Government, Fiscal Year 2002, Table S-8, 230, available at: http://www.gpoaccess.gov/usbudget/fy02/pdf/budget.pdf.

14. Glenn Kessler, "Now President Faces Tax Cut Test," *Washington Post*, 11 February 2001, A5.

15. Dana Milbank, "Budget Battle Will Test Bush Anew," *Washington Post*, 10 April 2001, A7.

16. Robert Pear, "Bush and Senate Budget Plans Differ by Hundreds of Billions," *New York Times*, 11 April 2001, 1.

17. Philip Shenon, "Showdown Looms as Democrats Move to Burst GOP Budget," *New York Times*, 19 June 2001, 14.

18. Office of Management and Budget, "Mid-Session Review," 22 August 2001.

19. Amy Goldstein, "Bush Backs Tax Cut, Blames Congress," *Washington Post*, 22 August 2001, A2.

20. Adam Cohen, "Who Swiped the Surplus?" *Time*, 3 September 2001, 30.

21. Helen Dewar, "Daunting Task Greets Congress on Return," *Washington Post*, 4 September 2001, A4.

22. Gail Russell Chaddock, "'Fiscal Discipline' Curtailed, Not Forgotten, in Congress," *Christian Science Monitor*, 21 November 2001, 2.

23. David Bauman, "Finding It Hard to Say 'No,'" *National Journal*, 13 July 2002.

24. Examples from Citizens Against Government Waste, *Pig Book 2002*, available at www.cagw.org.

25. Winslow Wheeler, *The Wastrels of Defense: How Congress Sabotages US Security* (Naval Institute Press, 2004), xi.

26. Estimates from Citizens Against Government Waste, available at www.cagw.org.

27. This quip is the title of one of the chapters in Wheeler's book.

28. Quoted in Wheeler, 37–38.

29. For data on the war on terror appropriations, see Congressional Budget Office, "The Budget and Economic Outlook: Fiscal Years 2007 to 2016," January 2006, 6–7.

30. Author's calculations based on ibid.

31. Mike Allen, "Budget Chief Predicts Deficits for the Rest of Bush's Term," *Washington Post*, 29 November 2001, A1.

32. David T. Cook, "Monitor Breakfast: Mitch Daniels," *Christian Science Monitor*, 3 December 2001, 25.

33. Mike Allen, "Bush Pledges Effort to Balance Budget by 2004," *Washington Post*, 17 April 2002, A6.

34. John Lancaster, "'Earmark' Attack Raises Hackles," *Washington Post*, 11 February 2002, A23.

35. Daniel Griswold, Stephen Slivinski, and Chris Preble, "Ripe for Reform: Six Good Reasons to Reduce US Farm Subsidies and Trade Barriers," *Cato Institute Trade Policy Analysis No. 30*, 14 September 2005, 6.

36. John Lancaster, "Federal Farm Subsidies Are Hardy Perennials," *Washington Post*, 2 October 2001, A6.

37. Ibid.

38. Griswold, Slivinski, and Preble.

39. US Department of Agriculture, Economic Research Service, "Farm Income and Costs: Farm Household Well-Being," 10 October 2004, http://www.ers.usda.gov/briefing/FarmIncome. This analysis is based on the annual Agricultural Resource Management Survey conducted by the Economic Research Service.

40. Data from the Environmental Working Group Farm Subsidy Database (www.ewg.org), based on data from the US Department of Agriculture.

41. Jeanne Cummings and John D. McKinnon, "Bush Budget Focuses on Homeland Defense and Economy," *Wall Street Journal*, 10 January 2000, A14.

42. Mike Allen, "Bush Calls Farm Subsidies a National Security Issue," *Washington Post*, 9 February 2002, A4.

43. David Rogers, "House Passes Massive Farm Bill," *Wall Street Journal*, 3 May 2002, A12.

44. Dan Morgan, "House Passes Bill Boosting Farmers' Subsidies by $31 Billion," *Washington Post*, 3 May 2002, A4.

45. Bauman, 340.

46. Mike Allen, "Bush Signs Bill Providing Big Farm Subsidy Increases," *Washington Post*, 14 May 2002, A1.

47. Jonathan Weisman, "Bush Goals Not Met in 2003 Budget Bill," *Washington Post*, 16 February 2003, A5.

48. Tom Miller, "The Medicare Drug War Escalates: Bush Opens Up a New Front—Comprehensive Reform," *Cato Institute White Paper*, 8 September 2000.

49. The story of Frist's ascension to the majority leader post is told in Major Garrett, *The Enduring Revolution* (Crown Forum, 2005), 265.

50. David Rogers, "Hastert, Frist Take Command of Mending Medicare," *Wall Street Journal*, 6 March 2003, A4.

51. Garrett, 251.

52. Robin Toner and Robert Pear, "Bush Seeks Medicare Drug Bill That Conservatives Oppose," *New York Times*, 24 June 2003, 18.

53. William M. Welch, "Conservatives Sound Warning over Medicare Plan," *USA Today*, 14 July 2003, A4.

54. Associated Press, "Bush Eager for Congress to Send Him Medicare Bill," 29 June 2003.

55. Robin Toner, "Changing Prospects for Medicare Drug Benefits," *New York Times*, 15 June 2002, 15.

56. Amy Goldstein, "Higher Medicare Costs Suspected for Months," *Washington Post*, 31 January 2004, A1.

57. This has been confirmed by an internal HHS investigation by the Inspector General's office. See US Department of Health and Human Services, "Statement of Dara Corrigan, Acting Principal Deputy Inspector General, Department of Health and Human Services, on Thomas Scully and Richard Foster Investigation," Office of the Inspector General, 6 July 2004.

58. Newt Gingrich, "Conservatives Should Vote 'Yes' on Medicare," *Wall Street Journal*, 20 November 2003, A20.

59. Garrett, 256–257.

60. Jonathan E. Kaplan, "'Me Too, Pal,' Says Bush, Hanging Up," *The Hill*, 3 December 2003. This story was corroborated by sources inside the White House and Feeney's office.

61. Norman Ornstein, ". . . and Mischief," *Washington Post*, 26 November 2003.

62. This story has been confirmed by multiple sources, including the

House Ethics Committee which meted out to DeLay no more than a slap on the wrist. See Garrett, 243.

63. The story of the House vote was adapted from Garrett, 254–264.

64. Ornstein, 26 November 2003.

65. Joseph Antos and Jagadeesh Gokhale, "Medicare Prescription Drugs: Medical Necessity Meets Fiscal Insanity," *Cato Institute Briefing Paper No. 91,* 9 February 2005.

66. Amy Goldstein and Helen Dewar, "GOP Still Seeking Afterglow of Vote on Drug Benefits," *Washington Post,* 29 February 2004, A7.

67. This number comes from the 2005 annual reports of the trustees of the Medicare trust funds, available at http://www.cms.hhs.gov/ReportsTrustFunds/downloads/tr2005.pdf.

68. Jackie Calmes, "Bush Finds Party Faithful in Ugly Mood," *Wall Street Journal,* 9 February 2004, A4.

69. Carl Hulse, "Senate Backs $318 Billion for Highways," *New York Times,* 13 February 2004, 16.

70. Dan Morgan and Juliet Eilperin, "Deficit Puts Brakes on Highway Spending," *Washington Post,* 2 February 2004, A2.

71. Gabriel Roth, "Liberating the Roads," *Cato Institute Policy Analysis No 538,* 17 March 2005, 12.

72. Amy Schatz, "Bipartisanship Cruises on Highway Outlays," *Wall Street Journal,* 18 March 2005, A4.

73. Jonathan Weisman, "In Congress, the GOP Embraces Its Spending Side," *Washington Post,* 4 August 2005, A1.

74. Scott Fornek, "Bush Signs Highway Bill," *Chicago Sun-Times,* 10 August 2005.

75. Weisman, 4 August 2005.

76. Ibid.

77. The average annual growth is calculated by fiscal year.

78. Joshua Bolten, "We Can Cut the Deficit in Half," *Wall Street Journal,* 10 December 2003, available at http://www.whitehouse.gov/omb/pubpress/bolten_commentary.html.

79. Ibid.

80. Garrett, 155–169.

81. Congressional Budget Office, *The Budget and Economic Outlook: Fiscal Years 2006 to 2015* (CBO, January 2005), 6–7.

82. The sum of the revenue and expenditure changes do not add up to the absolute shift in fiscal fortunes because of rounding.

83. Goldstein and Dewar, 29 February 2004.

CHAPTER 6—The Flaws of Big Government Conservatism

1. Jo Mannies, "George W. Bush Visits Grace Hill Family Center," *St. Louis Post-Dispatch*, 13 April 2000, A1.

2. Terry M. Neal, "Bush Unveils a Reading Skills Plan," *Washington Post*, 29 March 2000, A1.

3. Wire services, "In Speech at Retirement Home, Bush Urges Using $67 Billion for Medical Research," *St. Louis Post-Dispatch*, 23 September 2000, 20.

4. Tom McClusky, "A Chicken in Every Pot and Ten Thousand Lawyers in Every Garage," *National Taxpayers Union Foundation Issue Brief 127* (Update), 1 September 2000.

5. Richard W. Stevenson, "Republicans Can't Match Bush's Plan for Tax Cuts," *New York Times*, 16 March 2000, 18.

6. John D. McKinnon, "GOP Rank and File, Fiscal Conservatives Battle over Tax Plan," *Wall Street Journal*, 15 March 2000, A4.

7. Peggy Noonan, "Hey, Big Spender," *OpinionJournal.com*, 16 March 2006.

8. David Brooks, "The New Bleeding Hearts," *Washington Post*, 16 February 1997, C1.

9. Quoted in ibid.

10. White House Press Office, "President's Remarks on Labor Day," 1 September 2003.

11. David Frum, *The Right Man* (Random House, 2003), 59.

12. Ibid., 17.

13. Major Garrett, *The Enduring Revolution* (Crown Forum, 2005), 238.

14. David S. Broder, "Long Road to Reform," *Washington Post*, 17 December 2001, A1.

15. John Diamond, "Bush Allies Muzzle Language to Abolish Education Agency," *Chicago Tribune*, 20 July 2000, 11.

16. June Kronholz, "'Accountability,' Not 'Vouchers,' Is Theme of Education Plans of Bush, Democrats," *Wall Street Journal*, 24 January 2001, A8.

17. Fred Barnes, *Rebel-in-Chief* (Crown Forum, 2006), 165–166.

18. David Salisbury, "Federal Education Policy in the GOP Congress," in *The Republican Revolution Ten Years Later*, edited by Chris Edwards and John Samples (Cato Institute, 2005), 161–163.

19. Author's calculations based on *Budget of the US Government, Fiscal 2007, Historical Tables* (Government Printing Office, 2006), Table 12.1.

20. Fred Barnes, "Big-Government Conservatism: How George W. Bush Squares the Fiscally Expansive/Conservative Circle," *Wall Street Journal*, 15 August 2003.

21. Barnes, 176.

22. David Brooks, "The Savior of the Right," *New York Times*, 23 October 2005.

23. For an extensive and detailed review of the economic literature on this subject, see Daniel J. Mitchell, "Supplement to 'The Impact of Government Spending on Economic Growth,' Heritage Foundation Backgrounder #1831," 15 March 2005.

24. James Gwartney, Robert Lawson, and Randall Holcombe, "The Size and Functions of Government and Economic Growth," Joint Economic Committee, April 1998, 27.

25. You can calculate this by using the White House's own budget numbers. Take a look at the Office of Management and Budget's "Mid-Session Review," 13 July 2005, Table S–10, available at: http://www.whitehouse.gov/omb/budget/fy2006.

26. Ed Crane, "Memo to Karl Rove," *Wall Street Journal*, 18 April 2005.

27. Bruce Bartlett, *Impostor* (Doubleday, 2006), 202–204.

28. Quoted in Michael Tanner, *The Poverty of Welfare* (Cato Institute, 2003), 122. For a more detailed discussion of the unintended consequences of Bush's faith-based programs, see Chapter 6.

29. Brooks, *Washington Post*, 16 February 1997.

30. Noonan, 16 March 2006.

31. Jonathan Rauch, "Why Republicans Can't Cut Spending," *National Journal*, 23 January 2006.

32. Frum, 93.

33. David Maraniss and Michael Weisskopf, *Tell Newt to Shut Up!* (Touchstone, 1996), 110–111.

34. Data from Citizens against Government Waste and Congressional Research Service, "Earmarks in FY 2006 Appropriations Acts," 6 March 2006.

35. Richard Lowry, "Say It Ain't So: How the GOP Majority Lost Its Way," *National Review*, 13 February 2006, 35.

36. Jonathan Weisman and Charles R. Babcock, "K Street's New Ways to Spawn More Pork," *Washington Post*, 27 January 2006, A1.

37. Ibid.

38. John Cochran and Andrew Taylor, "Earmarks: The Booming Way to Bring Home the Bacon," *Congressional Quarterly*, 7 February 2004, 324; and Weisman and Babcock, 27 January 2006.

39. Congressional Research Service, "Earmarks in FY 2006 Appropriations Acts," 6 March 2006. This is up from 1.5% in 1994.

40. Lowry, 32.

Chapter 7—The Curse of Incumbency

1. James L. Payne, *The Culture of Spending: Why Congress Lives Beyond Our Means* (ICS Press, 1991).

2. National Endowment for the Arts, *2004 Annual Report*, September 2005, 25, available at: http://www.arts.gov/about/04Annual/index.html.

3. This is calculated by dividing the NEA/NEH budget by the total collected in income taxes. Obviously, this also assumes that every taxpayer shares an equal portion of the cost of this program. The more you pay in taxes, of course, the larger the share of the NEA budget you would shoulder, but it's unlikely it would ever amount to much more, even in the case of a high-earning taxpayer. So the numbers in this chapter are meant to be illustrative.

4. Data from the US Department of Agriculture, Economic Research Service, http://www.ers.usda.gov/data.

5. For a detailed discussion of this topic, see Daniel Griswold, Stephen Slivinski, and Christopher Preble, "Ripe for Reform: Six Good Reasons to Reduce US Farm Subsidies and Trade Barriers," *Cato Institute Trade Policy Analysis No. 20*, 14 September 2005.

6. Estimate from the Environmental Working Group Farm Subsidy Database, http://www.ewg.org/farm/.

7. Olson's seminal works on this issue are *The Logic of Collective Action* (Harvard University Press, 1965), and *The Rise and Decline of Nations* (Yale University Press, 1982). The discussion herein draws from both of these books.

8. Olson, *The Rise and Decline of Nations*, 37.

9. Jeff Jacoby, "A Ministry of Culture? Not in America," *Boston Globe*, 23 February 1995.

10. Ibid., 13–16.

11. Kenneth R. Weinstein, "Congressional Hearings and the Culture of Spending," *Heritage Foundation Backgrounder #1099*, 19 December 1996.

12. Chris Edwards, *Downsizing the Government* (Cato Institute, 2005), 16.

13. Demian Brady, "The 108th Congress: Rising Floodwaters or a Change in the Tide?" National Taxpayers Union Policy Paper No. 155, 5 May 2005.

14. Payne, 130.

15. See Alfred G. Cuzán, Richard J. Heggen, and Charles M. Bundrick, *Voters and Presidents* (Xlibris, 2003); Gregory L. Bovitz, "Electoral Consequences of Porkbusting in the US House of Representatives," *Political Science Quarterly*, Fall 2002, 455–477; Alfred Cuzán, "Fiscal Policy and Presidential Elections: Update and Extension," *Presidential Studies Quarterly*, 1 June 2000, 275; Sam Peltzman, "Voters as Fiscal Conservatives," *Quarterly Journal of Economics* (Vol. 107, No. 2), May 1992, 327–361; and William Niskanen, "Bureaucrats and Politicians," *Journal of Law and Economics*, (Vol. 18, No. 3), December 1975, 617–643.

16. John Berthoud, "Self-Limited Members of Congress: A Continued Commitment to the Convictions," *NTUF Issue Brief 128*, 29 August 2000.

17. Melinda Henneberger and Jerry Gray, "Bruised and Battered, GOP Rebels Learn Ropes," *New York Times*, 15 November 1997, 13.
18. Interview with Newt Gingrich, *Time Magazine* (online), 27 March 2006.

CHAPTER 8—In Defense of Gridlock

1. William Niskanen and Peter VanDoren, "Some Intriguing Findings about Federal Spending," presented at the Public Choice Society meeting of 11–14 March 2004.
2. All of the analysis in this chapter, unless otherwise noted, is based on the author's calculations from Office of Management and Budget data and Congressional Budget Office data.
3. Richard Vedder, "Divided We Stand, United We Fall," *Independent Institute Commentary*, 1 December 1997, available at http://www.independent.org/newsroom/article.asp?id=217.
4. Jonathan Rauch, "Divided We Stand," *Atlantic Monthly*, October 2004, 39–40.
5. Carolyn Lochhead, "Social Security Rehab Died First under Clinton," *San Francisco Chronicle*, 11 April 2005.
6. See National Taxpayers Union Foundation, Bill Tally database analysis, available at http://www.ntu.org/main/misc.php?MiscID=11.

CHAPTER 9—The Battle of New Orleans

1. White House Press Office, "Fact Sheet: President Bush Addresses the Nation on Recovery from Katrina," 15 September 2005.
2. Keith Bea, "Federal Stafford Act Disaster Assistance: Presidential Declarations, Eligible Activities, and Funding," Congressional Research Service, 29 August 2005, CRS-9.
3. Carl Hulse, "GOP Split over Big Plans for Storm Spending," *New York Times*, 16 September 2005; and Michael Fletcher and Daniela Deane, "Bush Tells Mississippi Planners: 'Think Bold,'" *Washington Post*, 20 September 2005.
4. Jonathan Weisman and Jim VandeHei, "Bush to Request More Aid Funding," *Washington Post*, 15 September 2005.

5. Andrew Taylor, "Price Tag for Katrina Worsens Federal Budget Outlook," Associated Press, 7 September 2005.

6. John Fund, "Hey, Big Spender," *OpinionJournal.com*, 12 September 2005.

7. Richard Wolf and Judy Keen, "The Buck Starts Here," *USA Today*, 16 September 2005.

8. Jonathan Weisman, "House GOP Leaders Set to Cut Spending," *Washington Post*, 17 October 2005.

9. Sheryl Gay Stolberg and David D. Kirkpatrick, "GOP Rebellion Threatens to Derail Efforts to Adopt Budget," *New York Times*, 15 March 2005.

10. Amy Fagan and Stephen Dinan, "DeLay Declares 'Victory' in War on Budget Fat," *Washington Times*, 14 September 2005.

11. Gail Russell Chaddock, "Cost of Katrina Relief Splits Republican Ranks," *Christian Science Monitor*, 20 September 2005.

12. For more details on the project see Taxpayers for Common Sense, "The Gravina Access Project: A Bridge to Nowhere," updated October 2005, available at http://www.taxpayer.net/Transportation/gravinabridge.htm; and Fund, "Hey, Big Spender."

13. Jackie Koszczuk and Isaiah Poole, "Budget Rebels Step into the Gap," *Congressional Quarterly Weekly*, 31 October 2005.

14. Robert Novak, "GOP in Turmoil," *Chicago Sun-Times*, 26 September 2005.

15. You can view the list at http://johnshadegg.house.gov/rsc/RSC_Budget_Options_2005.pdf.

16. Liriel Higa and Steven T. Dennis, "As Katrina Recovery Requests Pile up, Some Senators Join the Call for Offsets," *Congressional Quarterly Today*, 22 September 2005.

17. Shailagh Murray, "Storm's Costs Threaten Hill Leaders' Pet Projects," *Washington Post*, 22 September 2005.

18. Carl Hulse, "Lawmakers Prepare Plans to Finance Storm Relief," *New York Times*, 21 September 2005.

19. Murray, 22 September 2005.

20. Andrea Stone, "Republicans Offer Spending Cuts," *USA Today*, 22 September 2005.

21. David Wessel, "Bush Budget Aide Weighs Cut in Benefit Outlays," *Wall Street Journal*, 26 September 2005.

22. Christopher Cooper, "President Seeks Entitlement Cuts to Pay for Katrina," *Wall Street Journal*, 5 October 2005.

23. Author's calculations based on data from Office of Management and Budget.

24. Steven T. Dennis, "GOP Begins Effort to Cut Spending," *Congressional Quarterly Today*, 14 October 2005.

25. Larry Margasak, "DeLay Indicted in Texas Fundraising Probe," Associated Press, 28 September 2005.

26. Jonathan Weisman, "GOP Divided over Range and Severity of Spending Cuts," *Washington Post*, 6 October 2005.

27. Jonathan Weisman, 17 October 2005.

28. Zachary Colie, "GOP Bitterly Divided over Federal Spending," *San Francisco Chronicle*, 24 October 2005.

29. Carl Hulse, "Two 'Bridges to Nowhere' Tumble Down in Congress," *New York Times*, 17 November 2005.

30. Congressional Budget Office Cost Estimate, *S. 1932: Deficit Reduction Act of 2005*, 27 January 2006.

31. Scott Shepard, "Rank-and-File Republicans Seeking Election to Replace DeLay as Majority Leader," Cox News Service, 7 January 2006.

32. "DeLay Finished as Majority Leader," CNN.com, 7 January 2006.

33. Robert Novak, "K Street Candidates," *Chicago Sun-Times*, 16 January 2006.

34. Perry Bacon and Mike Allen, "Can This Elephant Be Cleaned Up?" *Time*, 15 January 2006.

35. Jeffrey H. Birnbaum, "Lobbyists Foresee Business as Usual," *Washington Post*, 19 March 2006.

36. John R. Lott, "A Simple Explanation for Why Campaign Expenditures Are Increasing: The Government Is Getting Bigger," *Journal of Law and Economics*, (Vol. 43, No. 2), October 2000, 359–393.

37. *Congressional Record*, 8 April 1957, 5258–5265.

INDEX

International Paper, 130
International Trade Administration, 56
Interstate Commerce Commission, 63

J
Jeffords, Jim (I-Vermont), 122, 199
Job Corps program, 28–29
Johnson, Lyndon, 4, 7, 29, 44, 49, 60, 134, 145, 147, 149, 151, 165, 195, 196, 198, 200, 201, 213, 223
Joint Economic Committee, 168–69
Jones, Rep. Jim (D-Oklahoma), 33

K
K Street, 56, 175, 176, 219, 220
Kasich, Rep. (R-Ohio), 52, 53, 55, 56, 57, 59, 63, 68, 72, 76, 103, 109, 113, 160, 213
    attempt to cut B-2 bomber program, 67–68
    budget battle (1999), 109, 112
    budget deal (1997), 121
    budget proposal (1998), 104
    highway bill (1998), 97, 100
    infighting with fellow Republicans, 57, 67, 97, 99, 102–3, 106
    Republican Revolution budget, 101, 104–5
    spending cuts, 57, 58, 63, 66–67, 70, 71, 79, 92, 111
    the "Zorro Principle," 56
Kirkland, Lane, 26
Klug, Rep. Scott (R-Wisconsin), 60–61

Knollenberg, Joe (R-Michigan), 177
Kristol, William, 85

L
Labor, Department of, 44, 71
Labor-HHS–Education bill (1995), 71
Largent, Steve (R-Oklahoma), 69, 74, 85, 87–88
    highway bill (1998), 98
Latta, Delbert (R-Ohio), 32, 34
Legal Services Corporation (LSC), 70
Lewis, Jerry (R-California), 177
Lindsey, Lawrence, 158
Livingston, Rep. Bob (R-Louisiana), 65, 66, 67
    refusal to terminate programs, 66, 67, 102, 106
Lott, Trent (R-Mississippi), 89, 124, 133–34
Lugar, Richard (R-Indiana), 104, 128

M
Mañana Syndrome, 29
Market Access Program, see also Market Promotion Program, 62
Market Promotion Program (MPP), see also Market Access Program, 61–62
Massachusetts Association of Nonprofit Schools and Colleges, 173
McCain, John (R-Arizona), 213, 220